Remaking Manhood: The Battle Against Dominance-Based Masculine Culture

Collected writings from the
Healthy Masculinity Movement
2017-2023

Mark Greene

Cover photo by Matt A. J. (Matt Johnson)
Remaking Manhood: The Battle Against Dominance-Based
Masculinity
Copyright © 2023 Mark Greene
All rights reserved.
Publisher: ThinkPlay Partners, New York City, NY
ISBN: 979-8-9870246-1-4
RemakingManhood.com

This book is fondly dedicated to my partner in life, Dr. Saliha Bava. Her powerful intellect and playful capacity to explore and co-create is why my work exists.

This book is also dedicated to my father, Arthur Wellington Greene Jr., the man who showed me how to be loved unconditionally.

Contents

Introduction
Screaming Bloody Murder and Other Unappealing Behaviors

To begin, I want to acknowledge that the term BIPOC shows up A LOT in this collection of articles. The term has increasingly come under criticism as being problematic, lumping a wide range of people together in ways that are not working for the folks it's meant to describe. In my recent work, I have shifted to using the term global majority as one that better serves to describe those who make up the vast majority of the world's population.

I have made the choice to publish these articles as originally written. They serve as a reflection of the ways in which language has and will continue to evolve. White CIS males like me must continue to learn and grow our understanding of ADEI, men's work, feminism, anti-racism work, and other social change movements. As new language emerges, there will be other language in this book which will want to be replaced as well. This ongoing evolution of language is a powerful reminder of how dominance-based cultures' presumptions of white and male privilege are deeply embedded in how we construct language and meaning. For people who look and sound like me, we either weed these presumptions out, or they come to define us.

***

Recently, I was invited to write a chapter on masculinity for the Routledge Companion to Masculinity in American Literature & Culture. My chapter is titled "Dominance-based Man Box Culture and White Supremacy." In writing the chapter, I dutifully mapped out the research and theories that drive my work on Man Box culture. It is an orderly and carefully constructed argument highlighting how Man Box culture directly fuels extremism.

Remaking Manhood The Battle Against Dominance-Based Masculinity, on the other hand, is something entirely different.

This collection of articles was published online between 2017 and 2023. Part of me struggles to acknowledge the stridency of some of this writing. The repeated screaming of "fire" in a crowded theater that is actually on fire.

This book is equal parts an exploration of male supremacy and authoritarianism and the quiet moments of being human in a word that continues to bring equal parts fear and joy. Ultimately, my work is about deconstructing dominance-based masculine culture.

Some of these articles draw on content from my book, The Little #MeToo Book for Men. Others were born out of the events of the moment. While they are not presented in chronological order, I have put dates on them to place them in the days either preceding the onset of the COVID-19 pandemic or after its arrival. A man like Trump becoming the president of the United States of America is proof the theater has been on fire for decades, if not centuries, long before the pandemic arrived. What exactly constitutes the theater being on fire? Epidemic levels of predatory capitalism, profit driven healthcare, environmental destruction for profit, systemic voter suppression, economic and sexual violence against women, BIPOC,

LGBTQI+ people, immigrants, other religions and so on.

Because these articles were originally meant to stand alone, summaries and explanations of the rules of Man Box culture repeat in some of these chapters. Given that our Man Box culture of dominance-based masculinity underpins every challenge we face as a species, how could such explanations not show up repeatedly? My gracious and capable editor Wendy Fox Dial helped me reduce redundant content where possible, but our Man Box culture is the repeating chorus to a strident and violent song. One that we have been singing for generations.

The articles here also mark my growing awareness that the twin moral catastrophes of white and male supremacy have always been rooted in how we teach boys to be men. Now that Trump's Big Lie insurrectionists have overrun the U.S. Capitol and many more extremists like Trump are tightening their grip on the Republican Party, I have little in the way of comforting news to offer.

What hope there is lies in the growing movement among men to break out of Man Box culture and create a healthy masculinity of connection. Human connection is the key to protecting our loved ones and preserving all we hold dear. It shows up in my book in the little human stories of pandemic life that are peppered throughout. But until millions of us men end our silence and actively take up men's work to replace dominance-based masculinity with a healthy masculinity of connection, we all remain at grave risk.

Which means, I suppose, we'll have to wait and see how this all turns out.

Mark Greene
March 25, 2023

A Dent in the Coronavirus Darkness

> This morning I cleaned the kitchen.
> You're damned right I did
> – March 27, 2020

We stay up late now, until one or two a.m., and wake up late. For me, that's around nine a.m. Late for you may be different. Every day when I open my eyes, I do a self-check-in, to see how heavy or light things feel. Do I feel well? Yes? Is everyone else in our little family well? Yes? Thank you.

I am writing from my family's apartment on the Upper West Side of our beautiful New York City. It is March 27, 2020, and the wave of COVID-19 infections is surging all around us. The streets are empty and silent but for the occasional wailing of a passing ambulance. The flowers and trees are also blooming. The sun falls in gentle arcs across green and growing things in the Central Park. Our family has been sheltering in place for almost three weeks now. As far as I can tell we have avoided contracting COVID-19 but it will take another two weeks to be absolutely sure, and by then we will have gone for groceries again, so, who knows?

So, I open my eyes. Perhaps I look at my phone. Perhaps I don't. Each morning, it's a choice. I look at my partner, asleep next to me. I listen to her gentle breathing. Deep. Clear. No coughing. Good. I listen for my son in the next room. Still sleeping. No coughing. Good. One cough in our house and I'm always there, a question in my eyes. "I just drank my water wrong, Dad," my son says, his expression a mix of annoyance and amusement as he turns back to his computer screen.

My heart feels the weight of it. Tens of thousands of people are waking up sick all across the city. Hospitals are completely overwhelmed, doctors and nurses are battling to comfort the dying, even as they are hamstrung by a lack of supplies, ventilators, and other support in the relentless war they are fighting for all of us. Our president is letting New York City fight alone.

This morning I cleaned the kitchen. It is a ritual for me. I like to think the distant sound of me stacking dishes, the clink of glasses, has meaning for others still half-dreaming in their beds. Dad's up. Dad's being Dad. As I wash and clean, I reach out tentatively and allow myself to feel the deep existential dread of the worst kind of uncertainty. Take the wrong step, touch the wrong surface, stand next to the wrong person, and fall ill. Or perhaps be fine, but infect a loved one. Maybe we've already made some terrible mistake, days ago with single small, everyday gesture. Touching a doorknob. Sorting the mail. In Western culture, we fear uncertainty above all things. Uncertainty is the devil, to be banished by schedules and spreadsheets and retirement accounts and sheer unrelenting determination. Uncertainty is to be planned away, defeated by vitamins, good grades, prayed away in churches, exercised into submission on jogging tracks and weight machines. We figure out how to stay safe and be 360-degree aware. We buy handguns and security cameras.

We teach our children about stranger danger. And just when we think we have it all worked out, a simple human hug becomes the life-threatening risk. In a world already dangerously devoid of authentic human connection, the irony is nothing short of brutal.

COVID-19 is the perfect storm of not knowing at every

possible level – at the interpersonal, the environmental, the political, the spiritual. And, as the universe would have it, all this comes with a lesson about how we have strayed. How we have lost our way. We are now forced to confront the single fundamental human truth, something that our self-centered culture of individualism has long sought to hide from us.

COVID-19 is our teacher. Herein lies the lesson. We are all interconnected. We are all part of one single, vibrant network of human relationships. There is no way that our political systems or societies will survive unless they are designed and built on a single central understanding. That we all rise or fall together. Instead, we have created a domination-based culture of isolating individualism, based on all the ugly predatory divisions of class, race and gender, we are falling and falling fast.

And yet, if we look, we see new human rituals are emerging all around us, crafted, in part, by the constraints placed upon us. In our homes as we shelter in place, on the streets as we pass six feet apart, so much more aware then we once were that another is passing. How is hello now? How is I see you? If you seek hope, then look to the positive rituals of connection coming into being all around us. They are powerful markers of human resiliency. In the weeks since we started sheltering at home, my partner Saliha and I have begun to cook a central meal every day.

I don't know when exactly it started, but it is our family ritual now. We share our ideas about spices and other details back and forth, little gifts, offered and received.

"What about adding some of this," and "Shall we use the nice serving dish? Yes, why not?" It's fair to say our lives depend on this, because, as hundreds of generations of our forebears will tell you, rituals are key in a world of uncertainty.

Late into the night, I pass my son's room and hear his voice. He's on his phone. "Good," I think. But the cadence is not conversational. It's something else. I come to learn that this fourteen-year-old boy and a friend from his high school are reading The Great Gatsby to each other late into the night. When this began, I also can't say for certain. It takes place well after midnight. I hear his phone on speaker, one voice reading, then the next. Sometimes I stand for a brief moment listening, but not for long. It is not mine to have, this story being handed back and forth in the night. "We do it to keep each other from going insane," he tells me. And there it is. Despite all that's aligned against them, two voices, here in New York City, telling a human tale to each other across the softly hissing ether; a ritual of connection born out of the chaos of uncertainty.

Notice and care for the smallest of your rituals. They are the reflexive human response to uncertainty and fear. Uncertainty's gift to us is the reminder that human relationships are the most flexible and powerful of resources available to us. Uncertainty is not bad or good. It simply is. What human beings create out of uncertainty can be so very beautiful. New rituals for a new world emerging right now all around us. It has never been otherwise.

Yes, Men Have Been Cheated

Why do so many men struggle to process
the message of #MeToo?
– September 23, 2018

Ask most men, regardless of where they are on the political spectrum, and they'll tell you. Something feels off. Something is not right. Daily we feel it, a surging dislocation, a weary dissatisfaction, and a restless sense of growing anxiety. It's the kind of discomfort you feel as you slowly realize the game is totally rigged; the game you've been bullied and shamed into playing all your life.

I'm here to confirm men have, in fact, been cheated, and they are starting to understand this in ever greater numbers. From some quarters, men's voices are angry and reactive. They say that men are not allowed to be men; that women have all the advantages. Others feel deeply uncertain, wondering how to engage, even support movements like #MeToo and #TimesUp without getting caught up in the binary crossfire of our culture wars. The fight for women's equality is creating an upheaval that is explosive in its implications for men's core sense of identity. #MeToo is a particularly timely earthquake, coming at a liminal moment in history when much of what once underpinned men's identities is collapsing.

Over the last few decades, even as women and their allies fight ever harder for equal rights, American jobs were shipped overseas and the American economy was subject to the shock and awe of banking and real estate collapses. Then came COVID and the waves of lockdowns and layoffs which continue to this day across the globe, making this an economic, a cultural, a political, a religious, and an interpersonal crisis for men. It's everything at once.

American culture is no longer able to provide a stable container for the culture of masculinity men have been taught to perform for generations.

•••

Our dominant culture of masculinity is often referred to as the Man Box, a term originally conceptualized by Paul Kivel as "the act like a man box" in the early 1980's, and further developed in the work of Tony Porter of A CALL TO MEN. Rule one of Man Box culture is that men do not express their emotions. To this day, we coach our sons to present a facade of emotional toughness and our daughters to admire that facade in men. Even in infancy, little boys are expected to begin modeling stoicism, confidence, physical toughness, authority, and dominance. The strong and silent type remains a central American symbol of "real manhood." When we make the choice to teach our boys to hide their emotional expression, we commit to raising sons forced to perform a narrow and closely policed version of masculinity that is both isolating and abusive. The rules of Man Box culture enforce hierarchical, command-and-control structures while suppressing or eliminating boys' capacities for connection, empathy, collaboration, innovation, co-designing across difference, and forming authentic friendships.

Which is why the nostalgia for a bygone 1950s era America is so compelling for some men. It was an America where women were forced to accept their status as second-class citizens. This provided the cultural container that made the Man Box seemingly rewarding for men, and its catastrophic personal costs relatively invisible.

With that retrogressive container failing, the brutal and

isolating costs of the Man Box become more evident to men, minus the countervailing benefits it once provided when women (and people of color, and LGBTQ people) had no choice but to do as they were told.

And even progressive men struggle with unintentionally internalized Man Box beliefs, feeling deep uncertainty as the generations-old container collapses. But the men who openly advocate for returning to a 1950s era culture? They are openly aggressive and enraged, because for them, inequality for women is central to the Man Box identities they cling to.

This liminal cultural space between what was and what is coming next is the source of men's surging anxiety. Long reliant on the command-and-control hierarchy of traditional masculinity, men have never been taught to manage or deal with uncertainty, while women, who have historically been subject to the whims of men, have had to manage it all their lives. Long used to operating in a culture based on power over others, any loss of that power feels to men like loss of identity. Man Box culture is so deeply ingrained in boys and men because it begins exerting its influence shortly after we are born. After a few years of Man Box conditioning, our naturally occurring capacities for emotional and relational connection, capacities that are our birthright, are already being stripped from us. The damage is done before we are even old enough to understand what is happening.

The list of central relational capacities that Man Box culture suppresses in boys includes empathy. The suppression of empathy is no accident. It is the suppression of empathy that makes any culture of codified inequality possible. It is in the absence of empathy that men fail to see women's equality for what it is, a simple and easily enacted moral imperative. Nor do we see our agency in racism, environmental devastation, predatory capitalism, the marginalization of LGBTQ people, the systemic abuse of immigrants, or any of our other social ills.

Yes, men are being cheated, but it's not by women gaining political and economic power. It's not LGBTQ, or any other acronyms out there. Its not fake news or #MeToo. We are being cheated by our own culture of masculinity.

The isolating impact of Man Box culture is at the heart of our culture's epidemic levels of male isolation, addiction, depression, violence and suicide. So, even as Man Box culture condemns our own mothers, wives, and daughters, to second class status, it is also cheating us out of living fully authentic, connected lives.

And until we wake up and understand that this is quite literally killing us, it will continue to kill us every damn day.

What is remarkable is that given the scope and reach of Man Box culture, millions of men continue to act from a place of empathy, fighting for connection, community and equity for others. But this happens in spite of everything Man Box culture does to them. Imagine a world where we encourage every boy's relational intelligence instead of suppressing it. Imagine a world without the Man Box.

Seeing the Man Box

For generations, American men have been conditioned first and foremost to win at all costs, forever struggling to rise to the top of Darwinian pyramids of male competition, framed by a simple but ruthless set of rules. But men in Man Box culture are collectively doomed to fail because the game is most certainly rigged. We're wasting our lives chasing a fake rabbit around a track, all the while convinced there's meat to be had. There is no meat. We are the meat.

Man Box culture is the equivalent of millions of gamblers sweating around a Las Vegas craps table, never questioning that the house always wins, even as our chips are slowly, inexorably taken away. This rigged game, a game we have collectively bought into for generations, is the unspoken and unacknowledged source of the male panic surging through our culture. I should know. I wasted decades of my life trying to perform a version of masculinity that turned out to be a trap. Man Box culture presumes to define the rules for how to be a "real man," brutally and universally enforcing these rules through bullying, shaming and violence. This enforcement begins so early for boys. Trapped in the Man Box, we live out our lives hemmed in by rules designed to cut us off from authentic, healthy personal and professional relationships with others. We are forever scrambling, conditioned to perform a version of masculinity that is fraught with unspoken anxiety, doubt, and confusion. Even now, as I struggle to get free, Man Box culture seeks to drag me back in. It eats away at my self-esteem, my sense of purpose and my hard-earned new identity, chipping away at me via the same poisonous messages that I have internalized for decades. "You're not rich enough, strong enough, or successful enough. You're losing. The people who love you are going to find out you're a fake."

I have to give the Man Box its due. This particular trap, this Man Box culture of masculinity we have collectively created? It is a real nasty piece of work. In the Man Box culture, boys and men police each other, dutifully enforcing the rules as part of their performance of masculinity.

"Real men" don't show our emotions expect for anger

"Real men" are heterosexual, hyper-masculine, and sexually dominant

"Real men" never ask for help

"Real men" are decisive and always have the last word

"Real men" are always providers, never caregivers

"Real men" are economically secure

"Real men" are physically and emotionally tough, we never show pain

"Real men" are sports focused

We prove our manhood, not by who we are, but by what we do; by what we earn, who we bed, how many points we score, who we dominate, how often we command, lead, fix and control. This becomes a never-ending treadmill for us, because in Man Box culture, the men around us challenge us to prove our manhood every single day. We are only as good as the last paycheck we cashed, the last women we can brag about bedding, or the last ugly wrenching pain we silently endured. This is the genius of the Man Box. We, as men, will never finish proving our manhood. We can only keep going, pushing toward an end zone that recedes before us; ever a few more yards away. Ever a few more runs into the bruising defensive line, spread out before us, other men, waiting to hammer us into submission, their eyes fixed on some distant goal posts we can never see.

Because it is rigidly focused on dominance, authority, command, control, and conformity, Man Box culture shames and suppresses the development of those relational capacities in boys that create meaningful friendships in adulthood.

In her book, When Boys Become Boys, Dr. Judy Chu of

Stanford University documents how our sons are taught to hide their early capacity for being emotionally perceptive, articulate, and responsive. Starting in preschool, our young sons learn to align their behaviors with "the emotionally disconnected stereotype our culture projects onto them." Chu writes, "Boys are taught to hide vulnerable emotions like sadness, fear, and pain, which imply weakness and are stereo-typically associated with femininity."

In her book Deep Secrets, New York University professor and researcher Niobe Way shares research from interviews with hundreds of adolescent boys. Way's research shows how our sons' joy in friendship and connection slowly atrophies over time, hammered away at by the message that needing or wanting close friendships is "childish, girly, or gay." In this way, Man Box culture relies on this drumbeat denigration of the feminine as its primary tool for policing our little sons out of authentic expression and connection. In a process that is constant and ongoing, beginning in infancy and continuing throughout our adult lives, boys and men are trained into seeing girls and women as less. The result is catastrophic levels of economic and sexual assault perpetrated against girls, women and non-binary people. Boys and men, our deep human need for authentic connection silenced, settle for the empty, surface-level interactions of the workplace and the gym. "Talk sports, cars, avoid anything real." When we fail to conform to the Man Box, we are quickly reminded to get back in line. What begins for us as external bullying becomes our internal voice. "I don't make enough money. I'm too slow, too fat, too weak."

The anxiety this internal voice creates is so consistent it becomes our baseline. We can never have enough success, confidence or security. There will never be enough of anything.

Maybe getting more money or sex will help. And back on the treadmill we go, bent on proving to ourselves we are "real men."

For the record, Man Box culture is not traditional masculinity. The two are not equivalent. Man Box culture refers to the enforcement of a bigoted, weaponized version of masculinity. While it interweaves some more traditional ideas of masculinity, Man Box culture demands we enforce the abusive tenants of masculinity extremists. The rules that say "control girls and women" or "don't be homosexual" are violence, pure and simple. This is a crucial distinction. For some men and their partners, traditional masculine values like being a breadwinner may be a good fit. Man Box culture rears its ugly head when its narrow rules of masculinity are brutally enforced, seeking to stamp out a much wider range of masculine expression and identity. When we oppose Man Box culture by performing manhood differently, men risk being ostracized, dumped, shamed, fired, beaten or murdered.

Even when we try our best to conform to the rules of Man Box, there remain thousands of ways to falter, to stumble, miss a step, or fail. The Man Box is not designed to let us finish, to let us win. It is designed to keep men policing and bullying and, ultimately, fearing each other. And then there's getting older. As we age, we realize with growing horror that we can't keep proving our manhood forever. Maybe the paychecks aren't coming, or our knees are failing, or the one-liners aren't working, or whatever. Eventually, the culture of masculinity we bought into dumps us by the side of the road and barrels on, fueled by a new generation of younger, more hungry men, perhaps even our own sons; new greyhounds to chase the rabbit, more hamsters on the wheel.

Our winner-take-all Man Box culture eventually delivers on its

22

promise. It has always told us what it is. Maybe we weren't listening? A few people at the top win, the rest of us are disposable.

A central component of 1950s America was a booming post-war economy and job security for men (not women), which supplied for millions of working men the central role of being a breadwinner. But the dog-eat-dog ethos of the Man Box ultimately led to an America where offshoring jobs, short selling subprime mortgages, and creating predatory healthcare business models are just examples of someone doing the Man Box right, robbing millions of men of our primary role as breadwinners within that very model of masculinity which makes being a breadwinner a central marker of our success. The result? Unemployment is linked directly to rising rates of suicide among older working age men. And so, as the curtain falls, aging American men are isolated and disconnected, left to express the only emotion we have ever been granted permission to express. Anger.

True to our Man Box training, we attempt to direct our anger at anyone other than ourselves. To admit we have been bullied and cheated would break every rule of Man Box culture. And most impossible of all, it would require that we acknowledge our own agency in all of this. It would require we admit that our collective obsession with America's cult of bootstrap individualism has ultimately failed us. It would require a reassessment of our priorities, our beliefs and our view of others. Most of all, it would require self-reflection, a capacity we were never taught to value, by a culture that does not care who we are as individuals. And when our anger ultimately turns back on ourselves, men commit suicide in ever growing numbers because we have no one to turn to.

How are men realizing we have been cheated? We look up one

day, and we discover we have been robbed of the authentic relationships and robust community that for hundreds of thousands of years, literally from the dawn of humankind, have provided human beings our purpose and meaning. Instead, we sit in our gated communities before our big screen TVs, distrustful of others and fearful of anyone different, anyone who is not us. We have been bullied by Man Box culture into swapping the fundamental joy of human connection for an empty, isolating, alpha male pecking order. We become like dogs, chained up alone in the backyard, howling and crazy.

The constant drumbeat of male rage that floods our media and surges up in our national politics is rooted in the collective self-alienation and social isolation that defines our Man Box culture of masculinity. The result for men is epidemic levels of divorce, depression, addiction, suicide, violence, and mass shootings.

We got cheated. Yes, we did. And everyone else is paying the price.

"Traditional Masculinity" Isn't Under Attack

Man Box culture is the real challenge
– February 26, 2019

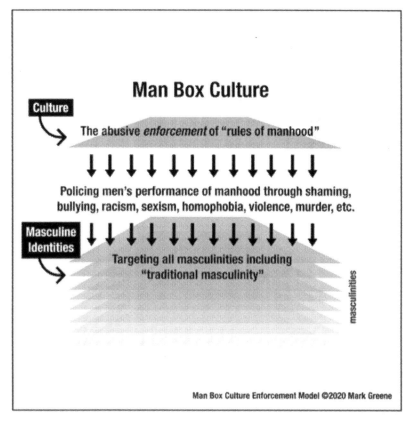

The American Psychological Association released its APA Guidelines for Psychological Practice with Boys and Men. Gillette made an advertisement asking men to engage and make a difference. In each case, the language they used could be characterized as pointing to flaws inherent in masculine identity. In the case of the APA, the language was "traditional masculinity ideology." In the case of Gillette, they used the term "toxic masculinity." Both organization's efforts were quickly reduced to "attacking traditional masculinity," which neither organization actually did, but there you have it.

A little unclear language and guys like David French of the National Review are off to the races. French wrote this on the APA's guidelines for the National Review, "In fact, the assault on traditional masculinity – while liberating to men who don't fit traditional norms – is itself harmful to the millions of young men who seek to be physically and mentally tough, to rise to challenges, and demonstrate leadership under pressure. The assault on traditional masculinity is an assault on their very natures."

Millions of what Mr. French calls "non-traditional men" most certainly do seek to be physically and mentally tough, to rise to challenges, and demonstrate leadership under pressure. Mr. French likely already knows this, and while Mr. French's crude binary may serve his political agenda, it harms the larger population of men, traditional and otherwise, by herding us all into an identity-focused grudge match over manhood.

The loudly trumpeted "assault on traditional masculinity" will play out in the coming 2020 elections. What's at stake is multi-trillion-dollar tax policy, women's rights, environmental policy, immigration policy, health care policy and more. What is not actually at stake is whether or not men will be able to be traditional. Plenty of that will be happening, whatever that may actually be.

While culture warriors like David French are happy to tell men that traditional masculinity is under attack, what they are unable to do is to clearly define the population they're talking about. For political binaries about traditional masculinity to work during the 2020 election cycle, all sides have to agree that traditional masculinity is white, monolithic, and conservative.

It is not. The full spectrum of masculinities is an exercise in nearly infinite variation and diversity. Just as there is a wide spectrum of masculinities within the subset of gay masculinity, so there is a wide spectrum of masculinities in the subset of traditional masculinity. The United States has hundreds of years of Latino American masculine traditions. We have Native American masculine traditions that date back thousands of years. We have centuries of African American masculine traditions. We have centuries of traditional Asian American masculine traditions. We have Jewish masculine traditions that date back to the Old Testament.

Need I go on? Okay, thank you. I will. We have masculine traditions among religious groups such as Southern Baptists or Unitarians. We have geographically located masculine traditions in places like Boston, and Wyoming, and South Florida. Hundred-year-old organizations like the Boy Scouts have their own sets of masculine traditions. Colleges have them. Sports fans have them. And all these traditions intersect.

Men socialized across the vast range of "traditional masculinity" are practicing very different versions of it, and because there is intersectionality across all of these traditions, traditional manhood becomes even more diverse still. Within these populations there are most certainly stark disagreements about politics, religion and even about what it means to be a man. Put simply, traditional masculinity doesn't exist. Traditional masculinities do, by the thousands. The rules of Man Box culture enforce a brutal and abusive caricature of what it means to be a man. They codify bullying and extremism, creating a culture of abuse that many so-called "traditional" men would and do oppose.

The American Psychological Association tiptoed up to the edge of naming Man Box culture with their language "traditional masculinity ideology" but failed to differentiate its singular agency and location (culture) in relationship to the full spectrum of masculinities (identities). Man Box culture is not traditional masculinity, it is a cultural agent, which acts on, distorts, and assaults all masculinities, traditional and otherwise.

When we advocate for a wide-ranging spectrum of masculinities, we undermine the gender binary which is foundational to the messaging of political and cultural extremists whose violent ideologies would collapse without the gender binary's simplistic ideas of what men and women supposedly are.

Our fight is not with masculinity, traditional or otherwise, it is with dominance-based Man Box culture, which is a danger to us all.

The Attack on Gillette's "Integrity" is a Larger Cultural Inoculation

How the integrity bind is used to silence men
in the era of #MeToo
– January 20, 2019

The Centers for Disease Control estimates that one in five women in the United States are survivors of rape or attempted rape. That's approximately 25 million human beings. And since many women do not report sexual assault, the actual numbers are much higher.

Against that backdrop the American shaving brand Gillette dropped an ad about men stepping up to challenge bullying and sexual abuse. The uproar has been significant. Gillette's ad has been attacked as cynical virtue signaling. Gillette's history as a company has been raised, bringing Gillette's "integrity" into question.

And so, Gillette's pricing, manufacturing and advertising practices are suddenly of great interest to reactive male voices across the media landscape. Issues that these same voices had no problem with, until it was time to call out the company's integrity in relationship to an ad that says, "men should step up more often, and in more public ways, to stop those behaviors we all know to be wrong."

And right on cue, we're embroiled in a national discussion of virtue signaling and Gillette's lack of continuity in promoting this kind of messaging. We're talking about how companies "cynically" take moral positions to improve their bottom line. What we're not talking about is how to end bullying and sexual abuse.

"Yeah, tens of millions of women in the U.S. are rape survivors, sure, that's bad, but damn, Gillette, you stepped WAY out of line. Dudes, your lack of integrity, has me furious."

I call this the "integrity bind." It's a core component of the full court press to push back against Gillette's message on bullying and sexual assault, and it's about much more than one company's advertising. The angry and reactive attack on Gillette's integrity is a cynical cultural inoculation, designed to reinforce the same bind for men in general. It works like this: If lack of integrity is the defining measure of why Gillette has no right to speak out on abuse issues, then lack of integrity also limits what we, as men, can say individually. If I am considering stepping up and calling out sexist behavior, how is my history, my integrity any better?

I'm not perfect. I'm a man raised in our dominant Man Box culture. From an early age, I was socialized to make fun of women and gays. I messed up a few times. Okay, a lot of times. I have no integrity, either. As such, who am I to stand up for anybody?

Our dominant Man Box culture begins impacting boys' ideas about masculinity from infancy. Man Box culture tells boys "Man up" and "Don't be a sissy," but what is actually communicated in those drumbeat messages is, "Don't be female or gay, because those people are less." Wrongly gendering the universal capacity for human connection as feminine and then shaming boys to see feminine as less is how we block our sons from the trial-and-error process of growing their powerful relationship building capacities.

During the years when boys should be expressing and constructing their identities in more diverse, grounded, and authentic ways, they are brutally conditioned to suppress authentic

30

expression and instead cleave closely to the expression of male superiority as identity. Locker room talk and the denigration of women become central to proving they are "real men" in their social circles.

We all grew up in Man Box culture. How could we not fail the integrity test? Bingo.

This integrity bind doesn't affect abusers. The continuity of their abusive actions is unbroken. This bind affects the millions of men in the liminal ambiguous middle, guys who are just trying to get their jobs done and take care of their families. Guys who remain silent in the face of the denigration of women, who choose to not confront bad behavior, who stay on the sidelines, because having grown up in Man Box culture they say to themselves, "Who am I to speak up?"

Let him who is without sin cast the first stone.

So, the question becomes how do men push past our deeply ambivalent awareness of our own histories having grown up in Man Box culture? How do we, as men, manage this question of our own lack of integrity when speaking out against abuse. The fact is, those of us who choose to speak up against bullying or abuse often do so, knowing we are hypocrites on some level, breaking with our own histories in that moment.

And this is why the full court attack on Gillette's integrity is such a central strategy in the larger culture war around #MeToo. As men, we will either fall prey to the integrity argument, opposing or remaining silent about messages like Gillette's, or we will encourage all people's and organizations' rights to evolve and take a moral position regardless of past actions.

In doing so, we grant ourselves the right to grow beyond our own histories, to stand up for what's right when we see abusive behaviors playing out. The world is burning, in part because of men's ongoing moral confusion. We can't remain any longer on the sidelines, avoiding conflict, protecting our status and position. We have to make some challenging and public choices and we have to make them soon.

What the future holds for our sons and daughters will depend on it.

Yes, Aunt Jemima is Some Racist Damn Syrup

Here's a little history lesson you
might find interesting.
– June 20, 2020

So, here I am, writing a quick article because people post on the internet declaring, "People are looking for racism where it doesn't exist" and, "Why are people attacking something as harmless as Aunt Jemima Syrup?"

Sigh.

This is from Wikipedia: "Aunt Jemima is based on the common 'Mammy' stereotype, a character in minstrel shows in the late 1800s. Her skin is dark and dewy, with a pearly white smile. She wears a scarf over her head and a polka dot dress with a white collar, similar to the common attire and physical features of 'mammy' characters throughout history. The term 'Aunt' in this context was a southern form of address used with older enslaved peoples. They were denied use of courtesy titles. A character named 'Aunt Jemima' appeared on the stage in Washington, D.C., as early as 1864."

The fact is, not enough white folks are learning about and acknowledging the simplest cultural stuff. Namely, how slave era images and language are still on our syrup bottles. It's the same with Uncle Ben's Converted Rice. Uncle was used for older enslaved men because they were not allowed by their white owners to use the term Mr.

Understanding how deeply slavery and racism is woven into

white culture is a challenging lift for us as white people. It's a challenging lift for me. The self-reflection piece is ugly and takes years to do. It's like peeling an onion, there are always more layers.

But the battle Black men and women, that all BIPOC (Black, Indigenous, and People of Color) have to fight for every inch of progress they make against entrenched white supremacist voices in our media, in our police unions, in Trump's goddamn White House is exhausting. So, thank you to those white folks among us who are doing anti-racism work and have been doing it for decades. Seriously, thank you.

As for the rest of us? It's time for those of us who fancy ourselves enlightened to get into anti-racist work entirely. To turn it up a notch. To get loud. To do the work to educate ourselves. And that most certainly includes me, who simply didn't know what Aunt Jemima meant until I bothered to look it up today.

Men's Anger and the Brutal Contradictions of Masculinity

Why men often default to rage when
they are challenged by women.
– July 12, 2018

Who men are collectively, and how we got to the place we are now is not a pretty story. We are suspended, rudderless, between our long history of male privilege and the newer, more equitable masculinities emerging from decades of social and economic upheaval. For this generation of men, there will be no quick or easy way forward. It will take generations for us to free ourselves from what was done to us, by us, for us, and through us, in the name of traditional American masculinity.

Put simply, how American men perform masculinity is killing us and all those whose lives we impact. Our mothers, wives, daughters, sons, our entire communities, men and women we have never met and will never meet are all paying a terrible price. Which is why this conversation about being a man has to happen. If we cannot do this for ourselves, straddling what was and what is to come, uncertain of simple moral imperatives, angry and defensive, then we must do this for those we love. We must find the courage to shift this culture for those close to us, for our children and grandchildren, who deserve to grow up in a world free of the brutal inequality that we, by our collective indecision, are maintaining.

As men, we must learn to deal with our discomfort because being uncomfortable is likely going to be par for the course for men for the rest of our natural lives, and how we process our cultural anxiety will impact our families for generations to come. Understand, my condemnation of our culture of masculinity is NOT a condemnation of masculinity. I do, however, hold us responsible for maintaining our bullying culture of masculinity if we fail to create something better.

The history of the world is one in which men have been taught to leverage our dominance over women – power granted simply by virtue of our being male. For my father's generation, men didn't learn to negotiate as equals in their personal relationships because they controlled the economic power in the family. Men didn't learn to deal with the daily uncertainty of not knowing because they were free to declare what and how things should be. Whether we openly use it or not, this legacy of privilege has been handed down to us.

Accordingly, for many of us, developing our more nuanced relational capacities faltered or failed utterly, preempted by masculinity's blunt assertions of dominance. And even when we attempt to navigate the complexities of equity in our romantic relationships with women, always behind the carrot lurks the stick of our power as men. It takes only the slightest bit of empathy to imagine the rage this would create for us were our positions with women reversed.

A cursory glance at the makeup of the U.S. Congress will confirm that men continue to hold the levers of power in our major institutions. Across the U.S. and globally, men threaten, brutalize, and murder women with shocking ferocity. Presented with these easily verifiable facts, men's defensive anger surges up from the disconnect between the privilege many of us continue to leverage and the calamity that is modern life. Surely, this is someone else's fault? Immigrants. Socialists. Feminists.

The wave of global trauma that dominance-based masculinity has subjected us all to has taken generations to form and will take generations to spend itself, if it ever does. For men and women alike, every action we take either adds momentum to this wave, or decreases its impact on the generations that will follow us. And because women's and even children's voices are growing louder and more insistent, men are slowly coming to a painful realization. There is nowhere to hide from the collective trauma all around us.

Whether it is video of gunfire in our schools or the cries of terrified children in Syria, our trauma is universal and ubiquitous. It is the air we breathe, it is the water we swim in; so universal as to be background noise, numbing us to the grislier realities of famine and war. If ignored, chronic trauma will be the defining legacy we leave to our children and theirs. If ignored, it may well be the end of us all.

The deep well of male loneliness

Male trauma is rooted in the collective self-alienation and isolation that is part and parcel of our bullying culture of masculinity. In her book When Boys Become Boys, Dr. Judy Chu of Stanford University documents how our sons are taught to hide their early capacity for being emotionally perceptive, articulate, and responsive. Starting in preschool, our young boys learn to align their behaviors with "the emotionally disconnected stereotype our culture projects onto them," and "are taught to hide vulnerable emotions like sadness, fear, and pain, which imply weakness and are stereotypically associated with femininity."

Our culture tells our sons "Don't be a sissy" or "Be a man," but the message is clear: Don't be a woman. Women are less. From infancy boys are taught to reject the feminine, constructing a version of themselves that integrates women's second-class status into their masculine identities. This drumbeat condemnation of the feminine is the perfect trap, cementing in place the interlocking double bind of misogyny and self-alienation that is the Man Box.

Niobe Way, author of Deep Secrets, documents how we shame and bully our adolescent sons into giving up their loving friendships in order to prove a destructive and isolating set of negatives. In Way's words, "Rather than focusing on who they are, they become obsessed with who they are not, they are not girls, little boys nor, in the case of heterosexual boys, are they gay. In response to a cultural context that links intimacy in male friendships with an age, a sex (female), and a sexuality (gay), these boys mature into men who are autonomous, emotionally stoic, and isolated."

The deep irony of all of this is that the men in Man Box culture don't feel empowered by male privilege. What they feel is trapped in silos of social and emotional isolation, under siege, left behind as millions of women and men rebel against an antiquated social contract that systematically cuts us all off from deeper, more authentic human connection.

The health impact

In 2018, Cigna reported that "Nearly half of Americans report sometimes or always feeling alone (46 percent)." Studies show that the health impacts of chronic loneliness are equal to smoking, causing much higher rates of diabetes, cancer, obesity, heart disease, neurodegenerative diseases, and more. Because our culture of masculinity suppresses our sons' relational capacities, it is a major contributing factor to the epidemic of loneliness in America.

At a time when boys should be expressing and constructing

their identities in more diverse, grounded, and authentic ways, they are brutally conditioned to suppress authentic expression and instead cleave closely to the expression of male dominance as the primary method for validating their masculinity. And so, men brag about hook-up sex and ghosting women, seeking to bond via the uniformly degrading and contemptuous narratives of locker room talk.

The result is millions of men who are reduced to being half anti-women and half anti-self, suppressing the authentic expression of who they are, even as they compete to parade their male dominance over women. The impact of women's steady progress toward equity on these men's anti-woman side, cannot be underestimated. Because women's empowerment is antithetical to how men in Man Box culture are conditioned to construct our male identity, millions of us are fighting to overturn the progress women have made. In this way, we fight to maintain the part of our identity built on Man Box culture, sensing the alarming lack of any more authentic identity to fall back on.

What's the way forward for us?

As men, we are confronted with a choice. We can continue to allow the bullying of ourselves and others to conform to the rules of Man Box culture, or we can start making space for a much wider-ranging set of masculinities. Millions of men are already doing this work. Rigid, limiting performances of masculinity are giving way to much more fluid expressions of gender, especially among millennials. Millions of fathers are taking on the role of full-time parents and primary caregivers. Homophobia, long used to enforce our domination-based masculine culture, is in decline among the younger generation.

But men are facing a double bind, the second half of which will require even more courage to confront. Many of us understand we must work to address the trauma created by a culture of masculinity that has clearly privileged us. It's a man's world, right? As men, we may even know that we cannot deny our part in creating everything from #MeToo to the ugly culture of white supremacy in Trump's America. But because our Man Box culture suppresses connection, we have developed none of the relational capacities needed to repair the damage that has been done in our names.

In order to break the Man Box cycle of isolation and abuse, men must take everything we have been taught about gender and flip it on its head. Which means we are facing the very things we have been conditioned to avoid at all costs. We must activate the parts of ourselves we have been trained to suppress. We must call on every relational skill we were taught to deny, previously degraded and wrongly gendered as feminine, including empathy, play, compassion, collaboration, connection, and that greatest of human challenges, bridging across difference.

We must rediscover our empathy and much more. We must rediscover nothing less than the art of being in relationship. We must come in from the cold and focus on growing our relational intelligence, learning daily to negotiate, explore, and play within our relationships in the context of a world that remains trauma-inducing and trauma-informed.

We can no longer avert our eyes from the deep disconnection our culture of masculinity has created in ourselves and the men around us. We can no longer cater to our discomfort, avoiding at all costs the challenging conversations required of us. We must do the work of connection and self-reflection, knowing all the while that the collective culture-wide trauma we seek to address will not likely be fixed or resolved in our lifetimes.

We must learn to sit with the uncertainty created by this lack of closure, not knowing what is emerging while the human heart does its mysterious work. In a world where men have been trained to fix instead of host, repair instead of engage, we must learn to hold the challenging emotions of others, possibly for years. We must understand the power we have when we listen. We must learn to sit with issues that will not be easily resolved and in doing so, perhaps, someday, resolve them.

Human beings heal in the back and forth of relating and connecting. We don't heal in isolation nor is healing something we apply to others; we heal in relationship. It can seem cruelly ironic for men to be asked to learn to connect after being brutally trained, all our lives, to disconnect, but the benefits of doing so are very real. When we learn to connect in the back and forth of sharing our stories, something remarkable happens. We're not alone any more. We re-engage with our larger human family. We become community, and any of us – regardless of our histories, our challenges, or our past sins – can begin this work.

It's time for all of us to gather our courage and connect. We must do this work for our children, our partners, our communities, our world, and ourselves. We must do this before it is too late.

Kamala Harris and Central Park Bird Watching

> Black people and the "you don't belong here"
> message of white supremacy.
> – August 14, 2020

On May 25th, 2020 a white woman, Amy Cooper, called the police on a Black man, Christian Cooper (no relation) because he asked her to leash her dog in New York City. At the same time, Trump and his political machine were questioning Kamala Harris' citizenship, and by extension her right to be a candidate for vice president. For many of us, after years of so-called birther attacks on Obama, it was an eye-rolling moment. Really? Again?

Whether for Christian Cooper, a Black member of the New York Audubon Society, or Kamala Harris, a Black candidate for the vice president of the United States, the underlying message is the same – "You don't belong here."

In a viral internet video, Amy Cooper is seen calling the NYPD and declaring Christian Cooper an imminent threat to her simply because he politely asked her to leash her dog, per park regulations, in a bird sanctuary. Her call to the NYPD took place on the same day as the killing of George Floyd by Minneapolis Police Department officers. Any call to the police by a white woman declaring herself to be under threat from a Black man in such a context should be seen as weaponizing officers against BIPOC.

George Zimmerman's reason for deciding to follow Trayvon Martin was that, supposedly, a Black child was in a neighborhood in which he didn't belong. Zimmerman then murdered Martin in cold blood.

Ahmaud Arbery, a Black man, was murdered in broad daylight for jogging "where he shouldn't be." Tens of thousands of Black men and women are pulled over monthly by police in America for being "somewhere they shouldn't be."

Which brings me back to Senator Kamala Harris. It took no time at all for Trump to call into question the citizenship of the Democratic nominee for vice president. Like Trump's attacks on Obama, his birtherism attack on Harris is utterly unsubstantiated. So, it seems crazy that Trump would do this again, against a natural-born U.S. citizen right? He must be desperate, right? Poor crazy Trump, right?

No.

Trump's birther attack on Harris makes perfect sense in the context of the white supremacist "you don't belong here" narrative that underpins both conscious and unconscious racism in America.

And while I can't say if Amy Cooper is a white supremacist, I do know that Amy Cooper called NYPD on Christian Cooper because she carries deep-seated bias about where Black people have the right to be. For millions of white people the simple answer is not where I am.

Millions of us have been brainwashed into automatically parsing our fellow Black Americans' right to be present, based on what neighborhood, store, office, or state of the union we are in. The most horrifying part of Amy Cooper's "you don't belong here" bias is how quickly it resulted in her quite conscious decision to call the police and declare Christian Cooper a threat to her safety.

For those of us white people whose deep-seated, gated-community, "you don't belong here" bigotry about BIPOC might be unconscious, it takes little more for us than waking up to this conditioning to challenge its ugly influence in our daily interactions. But that alone will not be enough. Powerful men and women in our highest positions of power are actively encouraging a race war. Millions of white Americans have been silent and on the sidelines for too long. It's a few hundred years past time to pick a side.

When Trump refers to (Black) "progressive" Democrat congresswomen in his tweets, saying they should "go back and help fix the totally broken and crime infested places from which they came" he is actively driving the "you don't belong here" narrative. In this moment, a direct line is drawn between Trump's white supremacist agenda and the death of thousands of innocents like Trayvon Martin. Boys and girls, men and women subjected to beatings, economic violence, imprisonment, and murder for "being where they should not be." Trump and the GOP level their birtherism attacks at Kamala Harris because it dog whistles white nationalist calls for a white-only America. Their "you don't belong here" message is leveled at a sitting United States senator, but it's meant to be heard by every BIPOC.

In stoking birtherism against Harris, Trump's white supremacist message to BIPOC is simple: If she doesn't "belong here" you most certainly don't. Turn down the wrong street. Jog in the wrong subdivision. Be at the wrong protest march and you may not live to see tomorrow.

Which means that we, as white people, can no longer sit on the sidelines. If we continue to allow a system of power that parses BIPOC through the lens of "you don't belong here," our hands are soaked in the same blood as Trump's white supremacist base.

Simply take a moment to try and imagine the pain inflicted by "you don't belong here." If your family came to America yesterday, an immigrant family like every non-indigenous family once was, or if your BIPOC family's history goes back more generations than most white families, imagine being told "you don't belong here."

Imagine being a Black man or woman and being told that the ground under your feet is not for you. That all the work and struggle and joy and pain of being human, of working to build a life, of finding meaning and hope and purpose does not matter because of where you are standing.

This is the message to BIPOC that Trump, the Republican Party and all the right-wing media would have us endorse as white people in America, when they push birtherism, be it against Barack Obama or Kamala Harris. "You don't belong here" is Trump's ugly white supremacist movement telling Black congresswomen to go back where they came from. It's telling immigrants, in a nation of immigrants they are not welcome, locking children in cages. It's telling Harris she is not a real American.

The visceral cruelty of Trump othering BIPOC's entire lives, to the degree that there is nowhere they should exist at all, is a deadly and dangerous act of violence. As white people, we can no longer hide on the sidelines, no longer avoid confronting this evil being done daily in our names.

All of this is informed by the indigenous people our genocide against indigenous people whose land we took. Which means white supremacy's notions of who has a right to be here has always been predicated on a genocidal lie.

Why Masculinity is "Whatever Men Can Get Away With"

When you have zero cultural limits on the assertion of masculine dominance, guess what you get?
– June 27, 2019

America's Man Box culture of masculinity enforces a performance of masculinity that has zero upper limits on the assertion of dominance. Man Box culture is designed to enforce a bullying, hierarchical social order. It trains boys and men to accept bullying from those above them even as they are encouraged to dish it out to those below. And how much bullying is enough? "Whatever you can get away with" is the rule.

Because Man Box culture glorifies bullying and dominance as the primary confirmation of masculine power and success, all men are invited to daily test the limits of what society will tolerate. Accordingly, we see dominance-based interactions play out in every aspect of our lives, from within our most personal interactions to the dynamics of our national politics. While millions of good men care about creating more compassionate personal and professional relationships, and so choose not to test the limits of men's collective permission to be dominant, the fact that this choice is an opt-out tells us all we need to know about what's going wrong.

In making dominance-driven masculinity our default, we have normalized the cultural force that underpins predatory capitalism, environmental destruction for profit, catastrophic economic inequality, unending wars, and all the other abuses of power that plague the human race. Man Box culture has given us a world based on creating power over others instead of creating power with others. It is a formula for our collective demise.

＊＊

For generations, our culture of masculinity has insured that the primary metric for our sons has been, "How much aggression can I learn to assert?" instead of, "How will my actions impact my personal and professional relationships?" If we fail to acknowledge that reliance on dominance is the metric we actively teach our sons (either by our action or our inaction), the violence perpetrated by aggressive and bullying men will continue to be framed by the poisonous and false assertion that "boys will be boys." Dominant and aggressive is not what boys are, it's what we force them to become.

Beginning in their early childhood we collectively teach our young sons how brutally effective aggression is, while also stripping away the powerful relational capacities for connection we are all born with.

Judy Chu (When Boys Become Boys) and Niobe Way (Deep Secrets) clearly document the process by which our sons are collectively conditioned out of wanting or needing close meaningful friendships and relationships. In the narrow confines of Man Box culture, our young sons are subjected to a drumbeat of bullying and abuse that eventually forces them to turn away from connection and close friendships into the open arms of policing and dominance as the only acceptable performance of masculinity.

We do this to them.

The resulting isolation fuels repeating cycles of rage, depression and aggression for boys and men. Our masculine culture of domination is an ironclad closed loop, an aggression trap that leaves our sons, husbands and brothers doubling down on the very dominant behavior that isolates them. The end result for men is crippling levels of loneliness, divorce, addiction, stress-related illnesses, violence and early mortality.

The result for women is sexual assault, second-class legal status, ongoing economic violence and a daily battle to assert their basic human autonomy.

While women also commit acts of aggression and violence, 80% of violent acts are committed by men. A conversation about male violence does not dismiss the importance of addressing acts of violence by women, but for the purpose of this conversation, we are addressing how we privilege Man Box culture and the resulting aggression it creates in men.

Phrases like "boys will be boys" or "it's just locker room talk" are examples of how we collectively shrug off Man Box culture. We hear President Trump declaring that his position as a celebrity gave him the power to "grab them by the pussy" and then we give him a pass when, by sheer dint of his abusive dominance, he dismisses the violent implications of his statement as locker room talk. This is because we have no collective consensus for dealing with bullies. The fact is, for generations, we have collectively accepted that in Man Box culture bullying is an empowering expression of masculinity. This is reflected in our collective inability to thus far effectively prosecute Trump's efforts to overthrow our national election.

And for this, we each pay dearly. Our culture, in failing to effectively challenge dominance as a central tenant of masculinity, abandons each of us, men and women alike, to individually set and enforce boundaries with every aggressive man we encounter. Which is exhausting. With some percentage of men, we must reassert these boundaries daily because such men will never stop testing our professional or personal vulnerabilities, seeking the weak points where they can push inside, overwhelming boundaries that represent a direct challenge to their model of Man Box dominance. A joke here; a small transgression there. It is a carefully modulated series of aggressions by which the rest of us are invited to take small steps backward and allow alpha bullies a bit further into our emotional and physical spaces. And while some women may practice this model of dominance, Man Box culture systematically conditions all men to embrace it, making this a widespread issue for how men see the world.

For the worst of these dominance-obsessed men, the successful suppression of other's interpersonal boundaries eventually leads to acts of verbal, physical and sexual abuse. This explains why #MeToo is so widespread and spans so many levels of abusive behavior. Men who embrace our Man Box culture of dominance are testing boundaries at every level with every woman in their orbit, modulating those tests from micro- to macro-aggressions depending on the context and relative power of their targets. If their micro-aggressions are challenged in a relatively equal power relationship, say in the workplace, these men will quickly backpedal, throwing up their hands, saying, "I was only joking." It is a form of interpersonal gaslighting designed to add insult to injury as they fade back and seek the next opportunity to test us.

Those of us who have been in proximity to a bully, for any period of time, carry the scars of this constant testing of our will to resist. It results in a lasting form of PTSD, whereby every new human interaction conjures fears of abuse for us instead of the miraculous possibilities of human connection.

My brother, just a year and a half older than I, became a textbook alpha bully. His violence toward me began when I was barely a toddler. I remember being with him in the baby pool. He would follow behind me, pinching me over and over. If I would cry to my mother, her response was, "You boys need to work it out." She was either unwilling to see her older son as a bully or, more likely, saw her younger son as weak. I couldn't have been more than three or four years old at the time.

Perhaps my brother had been sensing the growing acrimony of an impending divorce. Perhaps he simply didn't like competition for my parents' declining attentions. Whatever the case, his issues went unaddressed. For him the solution became venting his fear and anger at me. With meaningful parental engagement his solution could have been a better one. Instead, his bullying went unchecked.

What I was left with was a central memory of my brother in which he would instantly go from calm to raging if I provided any kind of resistance. It was a jump-scare explosion of rage and he used it to intentionally try to overwhelm my defenses, seeking to get me to turn and run. If I did run, his rage increased and he would go physical.

"You boys work it out."

This has been our collective response to the ugly pecking order violence of Man Box culture for generations. We turn away. We abandon our sons. We assume it will all work out.

I've got news for you. The boys will not work it out. They. Are. Children.

Instead, the alpha bullies will rise out of the vacuum of our inaction and failings, both as parents and as a larger culture. When we, by our inaction, accept the stripping away of our sons' joyful relational capacities for connection, and turn a blind eye to the drumbeat assertion of a masculine culture of bullying and dominance in their lives, we fail them in every possible way.

If we are to have hope for the future, we must create a new healthy culture of masculine connection or, better yet, a culture of simply being human.

Please understand, I do not condemn masculinity. Far from it. There are beautiful and transcendent expressions of masculinity playing out all around us. But if we as men cannot step up, challenge our bullying and violent Man Box culture, and create something better, then we are failing in our responsibilities to our families, our communities and to the millions of our brothers who are suffering and dying.

Our collective well-being hangs in the balance. Yes, create a culture that asserts the importance of toughness, strength, and leadership for girls, boys and gender fluid children equally, while also teaching the power of connection across difference, collaboration, emotional expression and relational capacities. Stop falsely gendering basic human capacities for emotional expression, connection, leadership or toughness. These things are not inherently masculine or feminine. To do so enforces a corrosive gender binary that herds our sons toward violence and isolation. For our sons, we can encourage and grow the joy they find in their close friendships, teach them their responsibilities to our larger communities, and model for them the long-term value of our own close friendships as people across the full spectrum of gender.

When we grow our own capacities for connection, we better

understand how to empower our young sons to willingly set healthy boundaries on aggression for themselves and others, relying instead on a much wider range of powerful relational capacities for creating rich, meaningful personal and professional relationships. It is through generative and life-affirming human connections with others that our sons' distinctive and authentic expression of self can fully emerge.

And in this way, we will change the world.

Why Some Men Still Fear a Wife Who Earns More

> Men, traumatized by our bullying Man Box culture,
> end up being equality illiterate.
> – October 6, 2019

Why are some men uncomfortable with a partner who earns more or has a higher level of education? I mean, that's more economic stability and resources for the family, right?

Man Box culture has conditioned generations of men to see themselves as providers, not caregivers. This central frame of Man Box masculinity falters if women earn more and, even worse, start demanding equal effort from men in housework and caregiving for children. The "men should be the breadwinners" frame was born at the turn of the last century when the industrial revolution shifted millions of men away from the farm and onto the factory floor, cutting them off from home life, redefining what had been shared work as women's work. Which suited men in patriarchal culture just fine. In this way, women, who were not allowed to earn, were at the mercy of their husband's benevolence, accepting whatever level of money, fidelity or compassion was offered.

Fast forward a few generations and women, who globally have come quite rightfully to associate education with personal freedom and autonomy, are pursuing education as a way to insure they do not fall prey to men's presumptions of dominance and authority.

Meanwhile, the "men as breadwinner" frame, which remains central to the rules of Man Box culture, means that men, consciously or unconsciously, associate caregiving and housework with a submissive status. This is why working women struggle to this day to get their husbands to do their fair share of housework. Thankfully, men's need to rely on Man Box ideas is beginning to decline. Many men are able to thrive in relationships in which we are not as economically powerful as our wives. Many of us are happy to support our professional spouses by taking up housework and childcare. In fact, we like the work.

I have a bachelor's degree. My partner, Dr. Saliha Bava has a PhD. My wife's achievements are a source of pride for our family. Her earned privilege in the world is well deserved. She is the primary breadwinner in our family and is the source of our financial stability. But this kind of educational and economic power imbalance between us, in her favor, is still seen as stigmatizing for men in our masculine culture.

Contrast that with the vocal pride of the stay-at-home dad movement in which fathers are primary caregivers. The level of pride and productivity in the home, celebrated by stay-at-home dads in the millions, is an option for any man who might choose that exhausting and rewarding work. But many will never see it that way. They are too invested in Man Box culture.

Men who remain deeply uncomfortable with the idea of having less economic/educational power than their wives often have no history that modeled for them collaboration between a man and woman as economic equals. What they likely saw was men exercising financial dominance over women.

Our dominance-based bullying culture of manhood models all relationships as inherently unequal. Man Box culture has forced generations of boys to adopt a version of masculinity that relies on power over others versus power created with others, meaning that millions of us remain "equality illiterate." So, men cling to symbols of gendered dominance in our home life. Doing housework is submissive. Therefore, women should do that. Even women who have worked at the office all day.

Meanwhile, many women have also internalized Man Box culture. Men who falter in their "breadwinner" role are shamed as not real men, sometimes by their own spouses. Retrogressive views of masculinity can haunt couples, even those who are modeling a more progressive power arrangement.

Moving to new gender models for earning, housework, caregiving and shared power will require a new way of looking at the value of all work both inside and outside the home. For partners, negotiating these shifting symbols of status will be an ongoing task as our relative power shifts over the course of our lives. Learning to do this shared power dance is crucial to allowing all to feel valued.

For the record, the implications of my saying all this at this very late date in the long history of patriarchy is not lost on me. "So, now that men are doing housework, caring for children, NOW it's time to acknowledge the value of that challenging work." It's got to be bloody aggravating for so many women, I know. Especially if they still can't get help cleaning the toilets in their own homes.

But this is where we are. As men, we need to set aside Man Box culture's destructive reliance on creating power over, and instead engage in relationships based on creating power with our partners, our communities and our workplaces.

Men must lead in ending our culture's toxic Man Box models of power and control. We must move beyond a culture of masculinity that is deeply isolating and unsatisfying for us and harmful to all those whose lives we impact.

Some Men Can't Stop Calling Assertive Women in Business "Bitchy"

What's behind our ugly cultural stories about
assertive women business leaders?
– December 6, 2017

Men who sexually harass women on the street, in bars, and at schools are abusers and bullies. When they do this in the workplace, they are also cowards, using the additional economic pressures of the workplace to force women to acquiesce, to tolerate, to signal acceptance of such men's sexually-located dominance.

The #MeToo movement is born out of women's rage against the continuing culture of unwanted sexual abuse in the workplace and every other place they turn. The challenges of being harassed on the street are potentially even worse in workplaces where a woman's financial security is at risk; where women being harassed can't simply flee the career opportunity they worked hard to access. Men like Harvey Weinstein or Donald Trump, or even Joe in the mailroom, are abusing women in spaces where women's careers, networks and family's financial security are at risk. The implication is, "Be a good sport, or you may be out in the cold." In that moment, sexual abusers are holding women's futures hostage. It is a coward's act by men who are beneath contempt.

Which brings me to the narrative in the business world that says women who assert themselves in the workplace are "angry," "bossy" or "bitchy," while men who assert themselves are simply being effective leaders.

Judith Humphrey, writing for Fast Company, has this to say about the issue:

During those moments when we are showing our strongest selves, women often are hit with ugly, critical comments. We are called "aggressive," "bossy," and "bitchy." Senior women I work with report they are at times labeled "ball buster" and "ice queen."

All these negative labels originate in the fact that women were brought up to be "nice girls." We grow up being encouraged to be cordial and pleasing.

Note Humphrey's use of the word, "pleasing." Now, overlay this "Women in leadership positions are bitchy" trope onto the #MeToo movement's explosive confirmation (yet again) of widespread sexual abuse in and out of the workplace. Now what does our woman leader narrative point to, specifically?

Even a cursory examination of the history of working women will show that early on, women were not only expected to defer to men as "natural leaders," they were also expected to dole out little flirtations and sexual thrills to their male bosses and co-workers. "Honey, get me some coffee. Honey, sit on my lap."

As women have gained more power in the workplace, this culture of sexually tinged obeisance has been driven underground. Human Resources policies preclude it. Our daughters are taught to refuse it. And yet, when sexual advances in the workplace get a resounding "No!" from women, or when women reach a level of success that they don't have to dole out the flirtation candy, men react in universally consistent ways. Men get nasty.

The universal "assertive women leader = bossy/bitchy" trope of the business world is a direct response by abusive men who have had their sexual dominance privileges taken away. "Women at the office used to be fun. Now they are not fun." When a woman's power and position preclude harassing her, it is the sin of sins. It is the exact moment that men's dominance is erased. Because of course it's sexual. Of course, that's where bullying, abusive men locate their dominance, in the intimate physical aspect of human interactions.

We all know about our "pussy grabber" in chief. About Harvey Weinstein. About Louis C.K. We know about Roy Moore. But as much as we'd like to just blame the most powerful men at the top, we all built this one, boys. Every catcall in the street. Every locker room joke. Every ass grab in the elevator, every leer, every rude laugh. Every "I'd hit that." We can thank our friends, our brothers, sons and fathers, ourselves for the rage that women feel as their careers, their bodies, their simple sense of personal joy are held hostage in the daily cat and mouse of our masculine culture of bullying and sexual abuse.

Face facts. Collectively? Men haven't contributed to creating a safer world for women; we've participated in sustaining a shitty one. And on top of it all, we have the unmitigated gall to declare we're frustrated that we don't get enough sex. #MeToo is an explosive rejection of men's ugly, brutal power games in the workplace and on the streets. Men's sulking resentment at having their power challenged is evident in the nearly universal "women leaders are bitchy" trope, and in the abusive responses men provide because women have the audacity to demarcate and enforce their own physical and emotional boundaries.

The wave of #MeToo revelations will continue, because men continue to deny our collective culpability. Just today a man wrote this in my feed on Facebook: "Locker room talk is just that. It is all talk and does not make you a predator."

Locker room talk doesn't make every man who indulges in it a predator, but it most certainly perpetuates a culture of masculinity in which violent predators can hide. That term locker room talk itself is designed to insulate the men who speak this way, as if they exist in some kind of magical man-only universe. There is no such space. Locker room talk is spoken in a world populated by the women and the girls who must co-exist with us, along with the words, ideas and yes, predators we grant refuge to. And as a man, I get to own my part in this. I get to own all the denigrating things I have said about women over the course of my life. I don't get a pass, and I don't get a #NotAllMen.

Until all of us take ownership of our own histories of abusive behaviors, take responsibility for what we have failed to do, and take action to stand up against the epidemic of public and private sexual abuse going on all around us, we will rightfully be held accountable for the men among us who behave like animals instead of human beings.

Patterns of Abuse Echo Plainly in the Kavanaugh Hearings

Republican senators went straight
to the tools abusers use.
– September 28, 2018

There is ample research to show our dominant Man Box culture of masculinity strips boys of their relational capacities, including their ability to have social connection and, by extension, empathy. It does so primarily by encouraging us to bully and police each other as proof of our masculinity.

Boys and men are forced into a pecking order of bullying and abuse and we never stop making each other prove it. As a result, we buy into bullying and abuse as central mechanisms for forming and expressing our identities. Our masculine culture of bullying links directly to more violent forms of abuse, including sexual assault.

As early as age five, I lived in fear of my own abuser. Other boys were often unpredictable and sometimes violent, but this one boy was intensely focused on me and me alone. His violent and unyielding presence in my young life meant I spent years – over a decade – carefully tracking his moods and daily movements and where his attention was directed. This abuser/survivor relationship requires a huge amount of energy and comes at a high price, stripping victims of our sense of identity, agency, and physical integrity, sometimes for the rest of our lives.

I cannot know who I might have become were he not in my life. I do not grant him power over who I have become, but he remains with me. And whenever I hear someone tell their story of abuse, I get ready for the backlash, both from the abuser they might publicly face, and in my gut, from my abuser, who remains with me as a physical presence to this day.

For abusers, the performance of rage at their own victimhood is the card they always play, performed as indignation at what they would frame as an unfair process.

Was it sexual assault my abuser subjected me to? I can't entirely say. Sexual assault, as we know, is about power. Intimate physical sense memories of my abuser remain with me to this day. After 50 years, I still remember how he smells. I still remember the pressure of his body against me. I still remember his smile as he closed in over and over again. But most of all, I still remember his RAGE whenever I stood up to him.

The fact that my own safety was left up to me to manage from a terribly early age tells us volumes about how boys are taught to become men in America. Be tough. Stand up for yourself. Man up. Fight back. It puts the onus on the victim. My own story is deeply informed by the Man Box culture we all are embedded in, and as I watched events play out in the hearing for Supreme Court nominee Brett Kavanaugh, I saw several very clear markers that brought back my own experiences.

•••

The hearings are over. Republican senators have gotten what they wanted, namely control of the Supreme Court. In order to get it, they wrested control of the Supreme Court from the rest of us. First, by blocking Obama's nominee Merrick Garland, engineering Kennedy's abrupt exit from the court, and then by pushing through Kavanaugh's nomination.

This is all textbook dominance. Voices in the hearings said over and over, "There is credible evidence of sexual abuse. We need a fuller investigation." As a result, Republican senators on the committee as well as Kavanaugh himself grew increasingly angry and reactive. This same pattern is seen whether dominance plays out in public or private spaces: the assertion of dominance followed by increasing anger if there is resistance. For abusers, the performance of rage is always the final card they play. In the case of the Republican senators, their anger was performed as indignation at what they would frame as an unfair process, but it was fueled by the same rage I always saw in my own abuser's eyes, triggered any time I began to resist. The rage exhibited by members of the committee and by Kavanaugh himself was not about fairness. It was about having their dominance challenged. This performance of rage resonates deeply with men who support Kavanaugh. For them, it is the confirmation of men's hard-earned right to dominate others they view as being beneath them – women and other marginalized people.

Though our culture will not permit a public admission of this, for the few men at the top of dominance-based masculinity's pyramid of abuse and power, an accusation of sexual abuse, of rape, is not grounds for dismissal; it is confirmation of their status. It is proof of their power. It is the reason they are to be feared and respected.

The performance of rage we have seen in the Kavanaugh hearings goes beyond simple anger or frustration. It included very literal warnings of more punitive actions to come. "You won't like me when I'm mad." And so, something new to that dignified chamber of the Congress has emerged here. The rageful tactics of abusers are coming out of the shadows and being integrated into political messaging. Rage in politics should always be seen for what it is, as should the smirking, eye-rolling, and dismissing of others that often accompanies it. It is the mark of abusers when their authority is being challenged. In public, they are intent on silencing civil public discourses. In the privacy of bedrooms and hidden places, they are signaling the physical assault that almost always comes next.

After Sen. Lindsey Graham (R-S.C.) exploded angrily during the hearings, many voices affirmed his expression of rage as being powerful leadership and fully justified. In a very calculated way, Graham and Kavanaugh used displays of anger and contempt to overwhelm the news cycle, pulling focus from testimony and questions delivered by calmer, more civil voices in the room. Additionally, they are seeding a narrative by which those confronted with women's stories of abuse are the victims of a "mob"; even as they undermine those women, our social and political institutions, and our efforts to legislate for full equity. When this victimhood narrative is seeded intentionally by presidents and Supreme Court nominees, we have stepped into a whole new level of disruption and manipulation.

Reliance on tactics like these are rooted in a culture of masculinity that trains us to respect anger and violence as the final arbiters of dominance for American men. Coupled with an Orwellian double speak whereby those who support white supremacist violence in the streets are the victims of "cancel culture" it becomes a toxic political mixture. Meanwhile, at the most basic level, the bullies on the playground continue to tell the rest of us what to do. "Sorry but this is how it works."

No, it is not.

Millions are rising up against the epidemic of abuse and violence in our society. Alongside women, good, decent men are working to end our bullying Man Box culture of masculinity. We are at a crucial moment in American history. As the stakes get raised higher and higher, we must call out and put an end to the blunt and bloody dominance-based culture of masculinity by which some maintain power.

When Men Say, "But I Am Not a Rapist"

> There will be no peace and no comfort
> for any of us until all of this ends.
> – August 19, 2019

As men, we can live in a world of sexual harassment and violence against girls and women and avoid being impacted personally. This is the privilege of being male. When this simple truth is pointed out to us, we become uncomfortable, even annoyed. As if we ourselves are being victimized because we're not being allowed to go on ignoring it all.

Nonetheless, men can live life untroubled by sexual harassment and violence against girls and women. All we have to do is one simple thing. Just stay on the sidelines. Be good men, sure, just don't rock the boat, just be quiet about it all. Then our levels of stress are pretty low. We're chill, right?

Sure, maybe sometimes we have to give some angry women some pushback. You know, assert that #NotAllMen are abusers and so on. We have to clarify, "I don't rape" or "I don't know anyone who rapes." But that's just us making sure people know we're good men. Then we can go back to ignoring this issue that we're not personally creating.

But one nagging question remains. What kind of "good man" gets annoyed when girls and women call on us to help? When a house is burning, do we stand by and say, "Well, I didn't set that fire?" The fact is there will be no peace and no comfort for men until denigration and sexual assault against women ends. We don't get to enjoy our comfortable lives until we ensure the lives of all others are equally safe and comfortable. Sorry boys, but this is how morality actually works. No comfort while wickedness abides.

Also – a culture that refuses to tolerate sexual harassment and violence against girls and women would also refuse to accept it against boys and men. Zero tolerance against sexual violence is a debt we owe future generations of boys as well.

The choice to take action can't be based on whether sexual assault will happen or has happened to a girl or woman we know. That's not an acceptable level of response because it grants us a vast range of inaction. "It hasn't happened to a woman in my circle" becomes our excuse to remain silent. And the reason it's a particularly bad metric for taking action is because we don't actually know which women in our circles are survivors of rape. It's a story our mothers, sisters, and daughters don't share with us because they are protecting us. They are protecting us.

The fact is all the women we know have been harassed. That's just baseline. So in our hearts we know our inaction on speaking out is already suspect. But whether or not we know a survivor can't determine the moral imperative here, otherwise it's back to self-interest, again. It's back to a world built around men and what we decide to ignore for our own comfort.

As men, we have a moral responsibility. We must stand up for everyone, everywhere and speak out against sexual harassment, violence against any human being, man, woman, boy or girl, gender non-binary person, stranger or friend. That is the baseline moral imperative that will define a good person.

To do less, makes you one of them. And they are not good people at all.

Electing Women Leaders Will Save Our Lives

Electing women leaders attacks the culture which
empowers authoritarians.
– May 19, 2020

Far too many of us are dying in America because we have authoritarians in the White House, the U.S. Congress and many of our state houses. When public health policy is based on dominance-based, authoritarian masculinity millions get killed. Not just by COVID-19, but by entire systems that value status and power over the well-being of all citizens. This is why it is key to our collective well-being that women are getting elected to more and more leadership positions. Gender and racial bigotry universally underpin authoritarian leaders' catastrophically bad public health policy; but a nation that elects more women empowers a new culture of collective action for public good. This new culture emerges in the moment women start to win in large numbers. While some women in elected office support authoritarian leaders the vast majority do not. If you must, consider it a numbers game. Read more about women leaders' more effective response to COVID-19 here: See "Why Do Women Make Such Good Leaders During COVID-19?" at Forbes.

When men vote for women leaders, it signals our shift from our dominance-based culture of masculinity to a more diverse and inclusive masculine culture of collaboration and connection across difference. The shift is happening, but it needs to accelerate because dominance masculinity's continuing chokehold on electoral politics has left us with unfettered predatory capitalism in healthcare, education, urban policy, foreign policy, environmental policy and more; the failings of which are painfully evident in a crisis like the COVID-19 pandemic.

Put simply? Authoritarian leaders don't give a damn if we die. Dominance-based, nationalist leaders in places like Brazil, India, Russia and the United States are letting COVID-19 decimate their populations. Diversifying our political representation by electing more women, people of color, LGBTQI+ people, non-binary people, will save lives and improve our population's overall well-being. And there's now rock-solid data on how diversification improves performance at every level. Organizations such as Deloitte have rolled out extensive research proving that organizations with women and other underrepresented groups at the very top leadership positions dramatically outperform organizations who are not diverse. Hint: Get diverse or watch your organization fail.

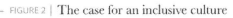

FIGURE 2 | The case for an inclusive culture

Organizations with inclusive cultures are:

2x
as likely to meet or
exceed financial targets

3x
as likely to be
high-performing

6x
more likely to be
innovative and agile

8x
more likely to achieve
better business outcomes

Source: Juliet Bourke, *Which Two Heads Are Better Than One? How Diverse Teams Create Breakthrough Ideas and Make Smarter Decisions* (Australian Institute of Company Directors, 2016).

Deloitte Insights | deloitte.com/insights

Based on the results of this research, we know more diverse

representation in elected offices will ensure healthier and more effective federal, state and local governance.

And yes, men in elected office who value women's equal agency and authority are also crucial to our collective well-being, but the election of women, people of color, gender non-binary people and LGBTQ people marks a much more fundamental shift than the election of progressive men. Don't get me wrong, I'm glad for progressive men in politics, but women's and other underrepresented groups' political ascendance marks our collective evolution away from our culture of dominance-based Man Box masculinity at a tectonic level. So, all things being equal, do you want to finally and completely shatter our retrogressive and deeply-ingrained American proclivity for electing authoritarian strong men? Elect women.

Lifeboats on the Coronavirus Sea

> Why do we take those we know for granted?
> – April 2, 2020

Why do we take the people we know for granted? It's a question I have asked myself often. Why do I do this? Is it just part of being human, that the miraculous can become commonplace with the passing of time? A new city, a new home, another human being? So wonderful at first, before the newness of them fades into the background noise of daily life?

My family lives in New York City. It is the city we love dearly. Yesterday, New York Governor Andrew Cuomo projected 116,000 coronavirus deaths across the state. Most of those fatalities will take place here.

A threat like this dials your thinking way down. Where I once reveled in our city's glorious sprawl of human complexity, now I track the specific square inches where that vast complexity intersects. A turnstile at the 86th Street subway entrance. The checkout at the grocery store. No, not the checkout, the credit card reader, where all the hands brush by. Places where the dead have been, or will have been, soon enough. The places a million hands touch.

A postcard for a casino in Atlantic City is waiting in my mailbox, addressed to someone who hasn't lived here in five years, offering a free bus ride from Port Authority. Wouldn't be so free any more. I wonder about the person who okayed this promotional mailing months ago, in a different world. Do they still have a job? I imagine one casino somewhere, still jangling and clanging away, its gaudy carpets trod by mad, grinning retirees who are forever fed up with being told what to do. Zombies in the coronavirus cyclone.

Then my thoughts slide sideways into politics, like they do a hundred times a day. I consider our president, who recently addressed doctors' and healthcare workers' lack of personal protection equipment here in New York City. "Something's going on … Where are the masks going? Are they going out the back door?" he asks on national television. Accusing embattled healthcare workers of black-market profiteering is pure Trump projection. Meanwhile, our doctors and nurses are dying on the front lines of a war being waged right now in the nation's hospitals, unable to get the masks and other protective equipment that would save their lives, much less ours.

This is how we are adrift in the lifeboats. Reviewing the string of catastrophic mistakes, small and large, past and present, local and national, that will eventually let the water come surging in. Looping from Trump's face, to credit card readers, to our children, to our lost jobs, to a $1,200 stimulus check that is out there somewhere, a token Lotto scratch-off winner from a lifetime of aimless scratching.

These are the kinds of thoughts that roil in our heads if we are the lucky ones, lucky enough not to have yet fallen sick. Lucky enough to be working from home instead of toiling in a warehouse on Staten Island to get someone an Xbox console in a day or two. We have the survivor's guilt, because we have eked out a way of staying home, because we haven't yet had to watch the virus kill someone we love via Facetime.

Stop.

Why do we take the people we know for granted? So madly in love at first. So amazed. So intoxicated. Later, less so, or worse, settling into indifference? How is it that my partner's magical way of being in the world is suddenly amplified by the possibility of losing her to a virus? Why do we so quickly forget? Why do we become numb?

This is the question for the lifeboats. For all of us bobbing on a vast sea of uncertainty. Suddenly, we are aware of how fragile it all is. The beauty of the young man who brought our family take-out food two nights back. He emerged out of the darkness on a still night. I, holding the door open as he approached our building, his face, beautiful, his voice oddly rich and melodic. For a moment, our eyes met. He, who is young. I, who am old. He, a delivery worker in the ghost city. I, privileged in my lifeboat. Some men my age are still delivering across the city late into the night. They all deserve so much better than this horror we have created, all of us.

The coronavirus is generating a level of complexity that I have never before encountered. It is shattering and shifting how we experience everything. Even the littlest of things. For years, in the spring months, when the windows are open, we have heard a woman teaching opera. She's not teaching any more.

Working here at my desk I would hear, echoing down the airshaft, a man singing, or a woman. It was a lovely, uniquely New York City sound. The man's rich baritone always brought to my mind Bugs Bunny. There's a cartoon where Bugs tricks a spoiled egocentric opera star into holding a single note until the entire opera hall collapses on him. There's a larger life lesson here, but exactly what it is escapes me.

Things have not fallen silent. I hear a new voice in the air shaft now, even as I am writing this. The woman upstairs is a schoolteacher. Before, I could hear her muffled morning routine before she hurried off to the school; now she is teaching online. I can hear her voice. It is the clipped delivery of instruction. "Here is the information. Here is our purpose. We are to learn this." Some idea, on some page, in some book, because life goes on and we are to do this work. I imagine two dozen other lifeboats bobbing, tied together by this monotonous common purpose, the old world, soldiering on.

Why do we take the people we know for granted? It is an important question, but now something about it nags at me.

We are so grateful when we escape the sinking ship as it slips beneath the waves on the vast ocean darkness. We scramble into the lifeboat and feel that dizzy relief as it lowers into the choppy waters. We hold our loved ones close. We move off from the stricken vessel. We are safe for the moment, and that is enough. Besides, our shelter-at-home version of the lifeboat is so full of ease and comfort compared to the millions of refugees surging across the world. Syria. Children in cages.

Jarred out of our day-to-day malaise we are awakened to what is not yet lost. Awake to what we are blessed to have for one more day. The voices from other rooms, as we shelter in place, can be so melodic and lovely. We have time. We have just a bit more time. I think to myself of the poetry of human connection and of the memories we make, are making now. I love my little family fiercely as I write this. Through force of will I bring to the surface my wakefulness and gratitude, taking advantage of the little nudge of self-reflection that catastrophic global pandemics provide us.

Why do we take the people we know for granted?

Like the Jews of the Old Testament, we have painted lamb's blood on our doors and are waiting for death to pass us by. We are awake in the night and holding each other close. This fierce love is an act of mindfulness fully awakened now for those we hold dear. Such a lesson.

But here's the problem. The question is woefully incomplete. The question isn't why do we take the people we know for granted. It never was.

The question is why do we take the people we don't know for granted?

Why this ugly, arbitrary drawing of lines between who is in our little lifeboats and who is not? If we don't get this singular question right, we will surely die. If not from coronavirus, then from the massive fires, or endless war, or predatory capitalism, or any other number of plagues born out of the "I got mine, now you get yours" mindset of America's obsessive cult of individuality.

When the sun is shining too many of us Americans give no more thought to the suffering of others than we do to a slight dip in the stock market. Millions suffer violence, hunger, sickness, homelessness, and death on our very doorsteps. In this pivotal moment in human history we are not called to paint blood on our doors and wait for death to pass us by. We are not here to escape Pharaoh. We are Pharaoh.

We have been fooled into believing we are a nation built on individualism. The result is that we sit behind our locked doors dying of loneliness and disconnection. And when the coronavirus comes to America's shores we have none of the collective resources we need to fight it. We are left to fend for ourselves, shocked in our final moments to realize we are, in fact, our brother's keeper. That it is in the vast interlocking puzzle of human community and interdependence that our salvation lies.

We are all part of a vast network of interconnected lives. For better or worse, the simple touch of a stranger's hand holds the immutable truth of this, the fundamental fact of being human. The coronavirus is posing the most important human questions, and if we don't start getting the answers right soon we will surely run out of chances to try.

Men and Masks: How Man Box Culture is Getting Us Killed

> We're more concerned about proving our manhood
> than about caring for others.
> – May 12, 2020

Man Box culture is a bullying, hierarchical pecking order. Boys and men maintain their status in the hierarchy by taking abuse from those above them and dishing it out to those below.

Paul Kivel conceptualized the "Act Like a Man" box in the early 1980s by asking high school boys what the rules were for being a man. It turned out the rules were pretty straightforward. They included:

- Hide all emotions except anger
- Be a breadwinner, not a caregiver
- Have control over women and girls
- Be tough, never admit self-doubt, fear
- Police and bully other boys who don't conform

There are a few more rules, but these are central, especially if you want to understand why men are doing what they are doing during a pandemic. Because Man Box culture is domination-based, it relies on constant internal policing and bullying to force conformity from men inside and outside the Man Box. All boys and men know they are being watched/policed.

The results for failing to conform to Man Box masculinity can be as small as micro-aggressive jokes, "What are you, a girly man? Haha!"; or escalate up to and include violence and murder. But the policing in male circles, even among longtime friends, is constant.

This conditions boys and men to be more concerned about policing other's masculinity and having their own policed then about caring for other's well-being in their communities. The degree of social disconnection this signals is amplified by our culture's cult of bootstrap individualism, going it alone and so on. Man Box culture's obsession with bootstrap individualism encourages contempt for collective efforts, for community practices, anything that might smack of caregiving or women's work.

Policing men into lockstep conformity in anxiety-inducing ways is how power moves to the top of our rigid masculine hierarchy. Meanwhile, those on top don't care whether those below them live or die. That's how they got to the top.

So, men in Man Box culture will not and cannot wear masks during a pandemic because it:

a) Makes them vulnerable to loss of their dominance status

b) Implies caring about others (feminine trait)

c) Signals a willingness to set individualism aside

COVID-19 has shown a spotlight on our failings across race, class, gender, politics, and society. Very clear data has been revealed about how female leaders, both internationally and in the U.S., from governors to mayors, etc., have kept their constituents much safer during the COVID-19 pandemic. Meanwhile, states or nations ruled by authoritarian male leaders are facing ongoing catastrophic loss of life. It's time to push back against Man Box culture as if our lives depend on it, because they do.

Male Privilege is a Recipe for Male Suicide

Learning to dominate those around us is also killing us.
– November 2, 2019

In Man Box culture, men are bullied into disconnection and isolation. Adolescent boys are shamed into giving up close friendships as being "girly or gay." Little boys are told hide their emotions. Children barely out of diapers are told to "man up" or "be a real man." The rules of Man Box culture require we spend our lives proving our manhood by doing, over and over and over. "Make money. Get women. Be the leader. Never show pain, doubt."

Man Box culture doesn't care who we are as individuals. It shames authentic connection, self-reflection, emotional expression, all the ways in which humans form connection and community. It is fundamentally isolating.

Male privilege exists in the Man Box, how much we are allotted depends on how well we can dominate others. We get benefits over women; we get the good old boys club and access to opportunities IF we conform and do masculinity "right." Which requires that we denigrate women, laugh off our pain, never show doubt, and always dominate those around us. While women don't have male privilege, they are permitted to form the social support networks, have more authentic conversations, ask for help from their networks. In Man Box culture, we shame men for admitting mental health or money problems, for feeling sad or lonely.

Because Man Box culture forbids boys from showing tears, fear, sadness, etc., we are cut off from the years of trial-and-error work we need in order to learn to create and care for healthy, authentic personal and professional relationships. It suppresses our capacities for forming the intimate friendships we need to resource ourselves during times of crisis. The surface level friendships we do create are always based on what we do, not on who we are. "Talk sports, cars, sex or money; never anything deep."

Without deeper, more authentic relationships, older white men like myself arrive at the last quarter of our lives with only the hyper-masculine rules of the Man Box by which to keep defining our self-worth. This should concern all men because sooner or later, we all age out. We can't get women, or earn money, or our health fails. And because we have spent our lives hiding our authentic expression, avoiding self-reflection, we can't suddenly create authentic intimate friendships. We just don't have the skills. So, we turn to expressing rage and blame towards others for where our lives have ended up. "I followed the rules! I did my job!"

When we hit the inevitable crisis that a lifetime in the Man Box guarantees, men are confronted with a choice. We can either break out of Man Box culture, or we can continue to double down on dominance. Millions of us, trained to never self-reflect about our own histories or trauma, continue down the second path, blaming others for where we have ended up. Eventually, angry and alone, thousands of us turn our rage on ourselves and commit suicide.

We have been sold the utterly false notion that real men dominate others. That single idea is killing us.

There is a solution. Men must simply admit we want and need real human connection. We can seek out organizations like The ManKind Project, or Evryman, or Humen. There are men waiting right now to help us do the difficult and deeply rewarding work that follows. We can seek out a therapist. Find self-help books. When we are ready, we can end our masculine culture of dominance over others and instead become part of a new culture of masculinity that values compassion and connection.

Begin this work early in life. Begin late. But know that no matter how old we are, it's never too late.

Ambiguous Grief and COVID-19

> Our American social system is utterly broken.
> – April 30, 2020

We are in our seventh week of sheltering at home here in New York City. The early, jangling alarm bell ringing days are over. Something larger and more difficult to name is taking their place.

Each morning when I wake, I check in with myself to see how I'm doing and more often these days the answer comes back "Not too good." More than I'd like, I wake up feeling numb, disconnected. Early on, I was experiencing shorter two- or three-day cycles of energy rising and falling. Now I sense a longer internal arc emerging, something very different. Perhaps I can only process so much alarm, political madness, lack of clear medical information, and existential uncertainty before my emotional responses just shut down.

It's the load we all carry during the COVID-19 pandemic; a potent mix of uncertainty, isolation, fear, and survivors' guilt, along with the rising wall of ambiguous grief we can't even name, yet.

In the beginning, the pandemic created a lot of nervous energy. Energy to get things done, to get supplies for the house, to seek information, to sound the alarm about how we had to #FlattenTheCurve. That early nervous energy has dissipated. The refuge we are taking, sheltering at home, is now the challenge we are facing. Like people stumbling into lifeboats as the ship sinks, we are initially so relieved. And then a week passes. Then a few weeks. Now, we're people drifting in a lifeboat. The alarming immediacy of the sinking ship is replaced with the deep uncertainty of being adrift.

After many weeks, our family is in a rhythm now. Getting up each day, cleaning, cooking, doing our work. Go to the store or don't go to the store. Walk a little in the evening on the empty streets. Meanwhile, just blocks away, healthcare workers continue to battle endless waves of COVID-19 cases in hospitals that have been stripped down and reorganized for a war. Doctors and nurses are dying. Patients are dying, unable to see partners or family members as the end comes. Tens of thousands of essential workers are working across the city, dancing with death in the empty streets. Communities of color, shouldering a majority of the essential work that keeps the city going, are dying at much higher rates, the direct result of how racism operates in America.

They are digging mass graves on Hart Island.

For those of us who can do little to help directly beyond staying home, we make purpose where we can find it. When our children ask for lunch. When the toilets need cleaning again, or laundry piles up, or work calls, or a broom is there leaning against the wall, it's a bit of purpose, but the larger picture? The larger picture we don't want to look directly at. COVID-19 has ripped the thin veneer of civility off American society, highlighting the brutal inequality, the savage divisions and sheer disposability of our fellow humans.

Every aspect of our American social order is broken, reduced to a shell by the cancer of our collective disconnection. Disconnection, and the systemic violence that disconnection always permits. Disconnection based on class, race, religion, gender, sexual orientation, and all the rest. Disconnection driven by our culture's cultish focus on the individual. The go it alone, never ask for help, man up culture of our dominance-driven masculinity. We have taken every aspect of our beautiful human diversity and created ugly binary frames designed to divide and conquer us, to isolate us, keep us separated, even in our own neighborhoods, giving rise to our peculiarly American epidemic of isolation.

The result of our deeply isolating culture being that when COVID-19 arrived, we had too few of the collective communal resources we needed to fight it. After years of ugly political binaries, we don't know how to act collectively for our own survival. In fact, we have contempt for that kind of thinking. We are caught in a web of divisive distinctions; a million more ways of marking and weaponizing difference. "They're not like me. They don't think like me. They don't act like me. They don't believe what I believe, so I don't care what happens to them."

It's the sickly-sweet syrup of hierarchy and illusory status fed to us at every opportunity from birth, suckled as we are on racism, sexism and all the rest. We have been raised from the crib on the mother of all binaries: that people who are different from us are less, and we've bought into it, hook, line and sinker. "So what if they don't have healthcare. We do. So what if they don't have housing. We do. People like me are safe. Those other people? They don't matter." And the list of differences we mark is so long, and so detailed, that not only does it apply to those outside our gates, it applies to those in our own homes, sitting next to us. We are disconnected from our own spouses, our own parents, our own children. And then we get to the last piece. We are disconnected from ourselves. Because hidden deep down is the ugly realization that we are different. Different from the brittle isolating stereotypes that we steadfastly present to the world. The false self that seeks forever to not be different, never different. Different from what?

At the heart of the churning, ambiguous grief finally, fully being revealed to us in the harsh COVID-19 spotlight is a voice deep inside us shrieking that something is terribly wrong in these lifeboats of ours. They are not lifeboats at all. They are coffins. They are isolation, and distrust and fear and control. The isolating result of a virulent and predatory social order that feeds us endless divisions along with a steady diet of toxic water and air, healthcare for profit, authoritarian governments, endless war and all the rest. COVID-19 has blown through our illusions of safety. There is no safety in isolation. The drumbeat pursuit of material wealth has become our funeral pyres. It turns out we are all connected, all our brother's keepers, and they ours. Too late we are learning this.

Too late.

The truths illuminated in COVID-19's stark, clear light have always been there, seen easily by those who bear the brunt of it all. Perhaps some of us need the metaphorical COVID knife to our throats to finally see these truths as well? Men and women dying alone because they are too virulently toxic to be near their own families. The sheer impossibility of a world without the very essential workers we can't be bothered to demand a decent working wage for. Lifetimes in which embracing anyone different from us is impossible. A world where our hatred and bigotry is a disease that is spreading unseen and killing us.

This is what lies aching at the heart of our ambiguous grief. The vast scale of our willful blindness. The growing awareness of the scope of change that our very survival demands. The epidemic of disconnection we must fight our way past, foisted on us by the bullies and the bigots who designed our racist and sexist predatory

90

capitalist dystopia. "I got mine. You get yours."

Try as we will, COVID-19 won't let us turn away from seeing it, now. It seems to me that some are in such a hurry to "open America back up" because all the isolating illusions they have so carefully constructed are at risk of collapsing. They fear we will realize that the normal they would have us get back to is killing us. That business as usual is a bloodbath.

So now, we all face a stark decision. Do we look at the virus ripping through our families and communities and say, "I'm okay with this body count, just get me back to normal." Or do we reach across the brittle barriers of race and class and create human community, finally? Do we find the humility to be inclusive, to humbly embrace the rich gift that is human diversity? Do we demand a human scope and scale to our political institutions? Do we make housing, education, healthcare a human right? Do we evolve? We can finally embrace the full range of what it means to be human. We can step out of isolation and into connection. We can leave our existential loneliness behind. Reject the death cult of status. Live.

But it's best we decide real soon. Because the lesson of COVID-19 is quite simple. Connect in fully human ways or our time as a species here will run out.

Diversity & Inclusion 101 for Men: Guys Telling Jokes

> Men seeing what might have been previously unseen
> can only be an advantage.
> – November 23, 2019

Thanks to research from organizations like Deloitte, men in leadership positions are coming to understand we must work to co-construct fully diverse leadership teams if we want to ensure our organizations will remain competitive. The dramatically higher productivity, innovation, and long-term value creation generated by fully diverse leadership is no longer even up for debate.

If men succeed in this new context, it is crucial that we each become mindful of the ways in which we have been conditioned to block the formation of more inclusive work cultures. Once we see the cultural landscape more clearly, we can stretch ourselves to become fully effective allies in the transformative work of growing diversity and inclusion within our organizations. Please note, although this shouldn't have to be said, not every aspect of our dominant culture of masculinity is problematic. Some parts create powerful and positive influences. But seeing what might have been previously unseen in terms of why men make the choices we make, can only be an advantage. This growth in "masculinity awareness" for men and women is at the core of any successful equity effort.

Which brings me to men and jokes in the workplace.

Last month, I traveled to Los Angeles (not the actual city) to speak with high-ranking male partners at an international ad agency (not the actual industry) about some challenges they were encountering. Men and women were reporting to the organization's diversity and inclusion officer that some partners were joking in ways that weren't landing well at all.

Case in point: a male partner opened a meeting by announcing that a female partner in the agency, one of the most productive members of the organization, was on parental leave and had given birth the day before. The male partner went on to note that the baby and mother were doing fine. Then he jokingly added, "And given what a powerhouse Alice (not her real name) is, I'm surprised she's not back in the office yet." He then went on with the meeting.

For some, this joke fell flat, and understandably so. To understand why, we have to consider the ways in which jokes are designed to operate. The reason the best jokes are funny is because they are designed to make us wonder what the intent of the joke teller actually is. It is in the duality of "did they mean this, or did they mean that" that the humor can arise for us. Was he complimenting Alice and wishing her a long and relaxing parental leave? Was he acknowledging they would all be playing catch up in her absence? Was he saying, "I'd prefer she be here sooner rather than later?" How could the others in the room really know?

Jokes do something else equally important. They immediately call up the context in which the joke is performed. In this case, this particular joke's context includes the two partners' genders, their relative levels of power, the historical issues around women in that particular workplace, the male partner's previous statements about parental leave policy at the firm (or lack thereof), and much more.

Which is why jokes that reference hot button issues like parental leave policy are, as a rule, a bad idea. Especially when

94

made by men with a lot of power at the top of the organization chart.

But my decade of researching and writing about masculinity also invites me to ask the question, "Why do men often feel the impulse to tell a joke in these moments?" The fact is, our dominant Man Box culture of masculinity has trained men to avoid expressing their internal emotional reactions or their ongoing challenges. The impact of this shaming of expression in men's lives is catastrophic, but one of the offshoots of this has been that boys and men are left with few options but to joke about challenging issues.

Which is why men almost always respond to even low levels of stress (ours or others) by telling a joke to acknowledge it. It's how men acknowledge our awareness of the challenges confronting us or others. It's a relief valve of sorts. A way to say, "Yeah, this is a thing, but, hey, I'm not worried." But here's the secret. In the moment we tell the joke about a challenging issue, we signal we are worried.

Regardless of their level of power or authority, my response to male leaders who ask if it's okay to joke about challenging issues is, "Don't do it." The questionable benefit of the joke regarding a hot button issue (can I thread this needle) is not worth the risk it poses for being unclear and potentially widely misinterpreted. To fully understand why the reaction to jokes will likely ALWAYS be unpredictable, we need to be attentive to the powerful role of the underlying context.

For example, a powerful male partner who is known to say repeatedly, "We want our employees, from every part of this organization to take their full parental leave. That includes the men. If you show up here before your allotted leave is up, I will personally be sending you home. We owe it to every person here to make sure they are free to commit to their family's needs equally. So, take your leave.

A leader who speaks publicly and repeatedly in this way has perhaps a bit of wiggle room around telling a joke about parental leave but ultimately, what's the point? Ask any marketing person and they will tell you, "Stay on message." A joke is the opposite of that.

Additionally, even a leader who has spoken clearly in these ways cannot know the level of anxiety others in the room may be feeling about their own parental leave options. What if, for instance, someone's spouse at home has a lot of fear about their partner taking the full benefit? That tension will inform how that team member hears the joke.

As men, even those in top leadership positions, we can often feel the pressure to fall back on coping mechanisms forced on us long ago by a culture of masculinity that gives us few ways to express the complexity of being human. When a joke comes up for us, we can learn to hit the pause button. We can check in with ourselves and ask, "Do I feel uncomfortable about this subject or event? If so, what is the source of my discomfort?" We can ask ourselves how exactly telling a joke would serve us (or anyone) and why a clearer statement of our intention might not serve us, and those we work with, better.

Partially Woke Older White Men, Part I

To the men who feel things aren't all that bad for women.
– December 18, 2019

Recently, I posted an article on Medium about the sexual abuse against reporter Alex Bozarjian by a male marathon runner as she reported on the race on live television.

As part of that article, I stated: "Meanwhile, the people we need to hear from are the millions of men who remain silent about our epidemic of abuse, rape and murder against women. We are living in a world where women are not safe. Ask yourself, what are YOU going to start doing right now, to change this?"

In response, a self-identified feminist man who has been challenging me in my networks for years posted this comment on the Medium article which summarizes this tweet stream. He said: "Mark Greene, seems to me you are engaged in a kind of fear mongering here."

I honestly believe he is well-intentioned, but I want to share my response to this idea. I want to respond to men who feel things aren't all that bad for women. Specifically, older white men (my demographic).

My response: Dear _____, I challenge you to do a gender reconciliation workshop. http://genderreconciliationinternational. org Go into that space and listen to thirty or more women tell their stories about being a woman in the world, today, now.

Listen as all of them confirm they are still afraid to walk the streets alone at night. Listen to stories of how watchful and careful women have to be. Listen to stories about what happened in their lives when they weren't careful enough. And even when they were.

I can't stress enough how women don't share these stories, especially with people who they know already discount the level of harm out there. And then there are the stories women have globally, which older white men like you and I are catastrophically oblivious to.

_____, I'm glad your life is comfortable and safe and that the women in your life are not currently being victimized. I'm glad for all that. But please don't discount the truth of the world just because your comfortable privilege insulates you from it.

I have a lot to do, and I can't keep taking friendly fire from partially woke men who feel the need to temper my views in order to keep their world more comfortable.

$%&#@!!?&!!

Partially Woke Older White Men, Part II

> "What is bullying, you ask? Oh, that's an easy one …"
> – December 18, 2019

A comment was posted today on my Facebook page by an older white man. (His post has some typos, so I have made some edits.)

He said, "I'm beginning to look at my fellow left-leaning friends, in real life here in ID, where tension (has) been high over a couple who sell their produce in the local farmers market."

"This couple has been accused of (being) white supremacists. It's possibly true. What concerns me is the vilification of people that don't automatically want to drive this couple from the market. A lot of talk about you must be Nazi sympathizer if you don't want to drive them out."

"It looks like bullying to me. It's got me thinking about looking through the lens of (what) is bullying in other situation(s). But I don't really have a good working definition of what bullying is. Have you thought about it?"

Yes, I have thought about bullying.

I want to approach my response by stating my own priority here; my hope that I can exhibit compassion for older white men. There are challenging assumptions in this man's questions, but please know I am not berating anyone. How can I not understand how he feels? He grew up in the same world I did.

My response: What is bullying you ask? Oh, that's an easy one. Bullying is a polite term for what white supremacists would do to you if your skin was not white.

Bullying is the result of those who believe in dominance as the right and proper expression of their advantages, be it class, race, religion or gender. It's not done to counter aggression; it's done to glorify aggression. It is domination for its own sake.

My work speaks extensively about how we bully boys out of emotional expression, using violence to slot them into hierarchical dominance-based masculinity. The alpha males of masculinity bully any who are different, any who are outliers. Bullies seek to punish difference and force conformity in a culture of domination. They express their own brokenness by hurting others.

But you are after a very different definition of bullying, I think. At times, you have seemingly implied that anyone who calls out male privilege, demanding that millions of silent men take action to end violence against women, feels to you like bullying them. And even more surprising, you seem to be hinting here that we shouldn't bully white nationalists, even though they are most certainly ready to bully all of us.

Rest assured, the only thing constraining white nationalists is that white supremacy is not yet openly the law of the land. But they would be happy to have it so. And then, I assure you they would happily kick in all our doors. Then you would see some bullying. But of course, it will be too late to do anything about it because we didn't want to, as you seem to be calling it, "bully" them at this earlier stage.

Also, your language, "fellow left-leaning friends." I can find you plenty of conservatives who would happily run white nationalists out of town. This is not a left/right thing. This is a fundamental moral issue. Racism is evil. Period. Full stop. When you frame opposition to white nationalists as "left-leaning" you do white nationalists' work for them, reinforcing a false political binary that serves their purposes. Be careful about how you use language. It is dangerous to chip away at moral clarity by inserting doubts.

White supremacists are not burdened by your need to question in these ways. They have no doubts as to their goals. They have children in cages at the border. Right now, while we partially woke white men have a nice debate about bullying. Honestly, I wish you could spend six months as a woman or as a Black man. It would clear up all these doubts you have about who is actually doing the bullying very quickly.

Ultimately, what I see here is white male discomfort. Millions of white men of our generation find all this upheaval deeply uncomfortable. We didn't grow up in the Great Depression. We didn't bare-knuckle battle to build unions. We didn't fight in the great wars. Men like you and I grew up in the easy times. When America was fast cars and dependable jobs. When white men like us just had to pick a good college. Today's constant calls to take action on behalf of others represent an intrusive discomfort in our otherwise comfortable lives.

It may seem easier to ask everyone to just calm down instead of confronting the ugly truth of white supremacy or the epidemic of abuse against women. But this is the work of white men like us. We must learn to lean into our discomfort.

The good old days are gone and they aren't coming back because the women, LGBTQI+ people, and people of color who made our easy lives possible aren't having it anymore. We don't ask Black men to lean into their discomfort because they live discomfort every day of their lives and much worse. We don't ask women to lean into discomfort because they live discomfort daily and much worse. Women, LGBTQI+ people, people of color can never ever step out of inequality/ oppression. White men like us can take a nice break whenever we like. No one is coming after us daily. We are not the targets. Yet.

My ask of you is to look at your own discomfort when others loudly oppose what you yourself suspect are white supremacists participating in your local farmers market. Is your discomfort about bullying? Or is your discomfort about your days long gone when you didn't have to care about things like this?

The world is in upheaval not because people oppose injustice. It's because we have white supremacists in the White House seeking to subjugate us all. Our right to openly oppose them exists for now. So, let's be really clear about what's at stake before we lose

this fight.

You want a comfortable world? Then older white men like you and I; we have to help make a comfortable world happen, not just for ourselves (we already have that) but for everyone else who does not. You want a comfortable world? Then wake up. Stand up. And fucking fight to create it for everyone.

A Simple Thought Experiment on White Privilege

This single paragraph settles the issue for most people.
– January 10, 2020

A lot of white men in the United States are suffering from unemployment, failing health, epidemic levels of social isolation and mental health challenges. A lot of white men are on the streets, victims of combat PTSD and economic disasters. Millions of white men are victims of our Man Box culture of masculinity that expects us to win every day and doesn't give a damn about us when we stop winning. When we tell men whose lives have fallen apart that they have white privilege, it can be difficult for them to hear.

I know white privilege is a complex issue, but here's a simple thought experiment on white privilege that any of us can understand:

Imagine you're in the U.S. You're driving down a country road in the middle of the night. You are far from home. Suddenly, you see police lights in your rearview mirror. You pull over and you look down at your hand. Imagine, in that moment, that you can choose to have any color skin you want. What color skin would you pick? If you choose white skin when dealing with the police, then you have just shown you know what white privilege is.

The simple fact is white people know the cops are going to be more careful about how they treat us. If that isn't a systemic advantage based on race, I don't know what is.

When Women Say "No, Thank You" to Our Request for a Date

Men can learn to see the lifetime of inflection points that inform women's choices about our requests for intimacy.
– February 5, 2020

Recently, a woman friend told me about being asked out on a date. It is a story from more than twenty years ago. She was sharing it as part of a larger conversation we were having about relationships. It's not a dramatic story. It isn't a story that was difficult to tell. Which makes it all the more instructive because it is so innocuous.

Twenty years ago, a man she didn't know well asked my friend out. "Would you like to go out to dinner?" he said to her. They were in the process of closing up at the end of the day at a conference where they and others had been working together. My friend said, "Thank you, but no."

The man then came back the next day in the course of their interactions and said, "Are you sure? I'm only asking for you to go to dinner." The implication being, "Just take a little time to get to know me. If it's not right for you, no big deal."

She again said, "No, thank you."

For most men, this may seem a very simple exchange. Stories like this can sting a bit, reinforcing our personal histories of rejection and the attendant sense of loss. But it seems pretty commonplace, yes?

Meanwhile, the incel (involuntary celibate) movement declares openly that men who don't get selected by women for sex have every right to be angry and violent about it. The rise of incels and other masculinity extremists means it's well past time for men to start talking and self-reflecting about what happens for us when a woman says, "No, thank you."

I mean besides, "Ouch."

What if boys and men, early in our dating lives, could learn to consider the vast landscape of reasons why a woman might say "No, thank you" to our offers of, requests for, intimacy? To begin with, we could ask ourselves why so many of us view the impact of a woman's "No" primarily through the lens of our own personal wants and needs? I've had this self-centered response more times than I care to admit. Especially when I was young. If men begin to question why we often react in this way, things will shift. We can start considering a larger set of issues. Namely, the lifetime of inflection points that inform a woman's choice (or a man's choice, or a non-binary person's choice) to say no to our offers of intimacy.

This is a conversation we really need to be having with other men, with our sons and with the women in our lives. The fact is, women's reasons for saying "No, thank you" may have a lot less to do with who we are as individuals, and a lot more to do with the culture of masculinity men have collectively created and are collectively sustaining. If we can, in good faith, make an effort to learn about the impact our culture of masculinity has on women's lives, we can dial down our reactivity when we get told "No, thank you." Learning about our culture's impact on women's lives is the personal work we need to do if we are to successfully challenge the incendiary agenda of incels and other masculinity extremists who think all women owe them sex. And THAT, we damn well need to be doing.

But any conversation about "women's reasons for saying no" must begin with this: No human being is required to provide a reason for saying no to another person's request for physical or emotional intimacy. "No" is its own reason. No is the alpha and omega of any human interaction. Learning to respect everyone's right to say no to an offer of intimacy is a crucial relational benchmark for us as a species. A relational benchmark that we have woefully failed to achieve.

That said, let's return to my friend's story. She and I talked about the brief exchange she had with this man. She then talked about why, in those days, she often said "No, thank you" to men seeking a date. In the initial moments, her reasons included:

1) I was about to move to a new state to start my internship

2) Dating had always seemed like a distraction from focusing on my education

3) I felt no strong attraction

4) I had been raised to be careful about men

The first three were clear and pragmatic reasons for a no, based on the life of a busy woman who was focused on her own priorities. This is something which, by the way, many men can never quite seem to fathom. Namely, a heterosexual (or bi-sexual) woman with no particular need for a male partner in her life.

The fourth reason she gave for saying no is seismic in its scale. It is the issue many women consider in these moments – safety. These four reasons together formed the context from which her answer emerged almost automatically as, "Thank you, but no," but there were other things specific to this particular man in these moments that she also recalled. These are things men often fail to notice but that many women see right away.

Take, for example, the circumstances in which he invited her to dinner. They were the last two people in the conference space for the day, doing final clean up, when he made his invitation. Whether he was aware of it or not, he was standing between her and the door. She had already been tracking the exits because this is what women do when they are alone with a man they don't know well, but now that he asked the question, she became even more aware of his position between her and the door.

"Thank you, but no," she said. She sensed that her answer didn't land well. Perhaps he was disappointed or embarrassed, but they didn't discuss it further. She made it her goal to finish and get out the door without delay.

When a man asks a woman (or anyone else) on a date, it is never a simple request. There is no such thing as "just dinner." When we make such an invitation, we are asking another person to be open to possible emotional or physical intimacy. Because it's about intimacy, it activates each person's histories, both good and bad. These histories can include past lovers, family relationships, friend's experiences, work relationships, momentary experiences on the street, and what we witness as children; literally every relational moment that has led up to now. Our histories of sexual or relational trauma leap to the forefront immediately. All of this happens in an instant.

When a woman answers "No, thank you," it could be the result of a previous ugly interaction between her and a man we will never meet; a man who created an inflection point in this person's life that informs how she calculates her response to men seeking intimacy.

And while these kinds of previous bad interactions can be huge, up to and including domestic violence or rape, they can also be smaller than that. They can be a single bad interaction, one small ugly moment.

And before we say, "But I'm not the guy who did that," we need to take ownership of something that many of us angrily refuse to accept. On a very real level, we are that guy. A lot of the deeply negative inflection points that inform women's views on intimacy are born out of our dominance-based Man Box culture of masculinity. This bullying and abusive culture of masculinity continues to exist because men, in general, have not demanded we create something better.

Every day we collectively fail to stand up to the very public harassment and abuse that the worst among us heap on women; harassment the rest often witness but collectively fail to challenge in any effective way. Things like locker room talk, catcalling, rape jokes; the daily denigrations of women that are so deeply embedded in how we've all been taught to perform masculinity. The use of "bitch" and "pussy" as the way to insult other boys and men. The nasty ways we talk about women behind their backs. The way we encourage each other to have contempt for women even as we seek sexual intimacy with them. "Yeah, I'd hit that," and so on.

Abusive, harassing men do not represent the majority of us, not by a long shot. But because millions of the rest of us stay silent, we allow a smaller population of bullying alpha males to define masculinity as a culture of aggressive dominance. We help sustain a world where the worst among us feel empowered to grope women, rage at women, attack women and degrade women publicly. We make a world where a man like Donald Trump can feel perfectly comfortable saying "I moved on her like a bitch" in casual conversation. We create a world that is safe for incels, MRAs and MGTOWs (Men's Rights Activists and Men Going Their Own Way) but not for the women they stalk, troll and assault. In this way, all of us create the world of ugly inflection points for women that result in "No, thank you" being many women's default response.

Even our very invitations are a source of stress and anxiety for women. Too many women have turned down a request to go on a date, and then had a man who was friendly a moment before become abusive, revealing his reactive response to her decision in a flash. "Why are you so stuck up?" he might say. A woman's "No, thank you" can instantly result in an alarming level of reactivity and aggression from men, an utter failure of emotional self-regulation. Maybe the man gets insistent. "I'm only asking for dinner." Or he gets hurt, crestfallen and sad in an ongoing way. Or maybe something truly terrible happens. Assault. Rape.

The price women pay for being asked out and simply saying "No, thank you," the resulting emotional work required of them by men who react badly, can be an exhausting inflection point that impacts every interaction thereafter, informing women's future choices. An abusive response to a "No, thank you" need only happen once or twice for a human being to remain forever wary of that question over the course of their lifetime. The joy of connection and discovery is suddenly replaced by being so very careful. A woman might then dress intentionally to deflect attention. She might hide her beauty and joy. She might avoid eye contact, avoid the gaze of men. Many women are already making these choices. And it's our fault.

As I said, the man in my friend's story approached her again the next day after she had said "Thanks, but no." When he added, "I'm only asking you to go to dinner," the implication was, "Give me a chance. I can change your mind." For my friend, that hint of I can change your mind cemented her choice to say no. This is because it carried the suggestion that perhaps she didn't know her own mind on the matter of choosing a potential partner or even wanting one at all. It was a diminution of her agency. In asking a second time, he failed to consider her context, her history, her professional and personal priorities, her position and her hard-earned authority in the world. In that moment, he didn't notice he was again blocking the door.

Like so many women, my friend grew up in a world full of warnings. Always be careful around men. Be careful about how you walk down the street. Be careful about your supervisors, your professors, your friends and your own way of showing up in the world. Get your education. Get your own agency. Don't leave your future in the hands of a man, or you will be sorry. You will be lost. My friend saw the reasons for these warnings play out over and over again in the casual displays of power by men who were so deeply invested in patriarchy that the harm they regularly did to women seemed simply to be within their rights as men.

Which brings me to the growing educational disparity between men and women. So-called men's rights advocates say women graduating from college at higher rates and with higher-level degrees is proof that the educational system has a built-in bias against boys and men. I would suggest a dramatically different frame. Women are more committed to the hard work of getting an education. And for good reason. They are pursuing education globally to whatever degree is available to them because it puts them on a path to liberation from controlling men. They all know this. Education, and the economic power that results, is freedom for women. They know that education will give them agency and financial power in a world where men STILL cannot be trusted to treat them as equals. Education is a path to autonomy for women. It is a path to being able to say, "Thank you, but no."

This speaks to a central, crucial metric for heterosexual women when considering a date. Would this guy encourage my professional and personal independence or would he seek to limit it? It is a question that plays out daily between men and women in both personal and professional relationships. For men, it is critical that we acknowledge the damage we have done collectively to women's careers, agency, and aspirations and are still doing right up to the present day. To our lasting shame, we continue to collectively give women a good reason to be wary of controlling men.

How men view women's equity in our romantic relationships shows up in big ways, such as whether both careers are viewed as equally important, and in small ways, such as who gets to finish speaking or gets spoken over. A woman who is tracking these issues can make a fairly quick predictive analysis based solely on how we ask her to go on a date. This metric includes how we accept her answer. Being emotionally reactive to a "No, thank you," is a huge red flag. Failing to take a no, regardless of how polished and charming we are in refusing to do so, is also a very bad sign.

More importantly, a woman who is tracking power in relationships, who is tracking how we might view gender equality, will look for us to acknowledge our own goals and aspirations as negotiable. She will look to see how we negotiate over even small

112

things, acknowledging the back and forth of balanced power in modern relationships. She will look to see how we co-create, neither seeking total control nor abdicating it. And we should be tracking these issues as well. Collectively, men have yet to transcend our archaic domination-based culture of masculinity. It is a culture that contributes to our own deep isolation and trauma while creating epidemic levels of economic and sexual violence against women.

If enough men chose to, we could end dominance-based masculinity tomorrow. If men chose to end our collective silence on women's rights, universal equity for women would be the law of the land. This is the amount of power we hold but fail to exercise, even on behalf of the girls and women close to us. We continue to blithely deny the real and present impact of patriarchy because it suits us to do so, blocking the door over and over again, without even caring to notice that we are doing so. Yes, men live in fear of domination and violence, too, but women live in fear of violence by men. Men commit 80% of all violent acts. Our refusal to see the full context of women's lives erases women's lived experiences; forever putting our own wants and needs above theirs.

Women are becoming more powerful. They and the men who are their allies are creating a world where abusive men are being challenged. This is leading to a crisis in masculinity. Angry, retrogressive voices are calling for open war against women, LGBTQ people, people of color, immigrants, religious minorities and others, and the outcome of this battle is by no means guaranteed to go well. Things could just as easily go very badly for us all.

Incels and other masculine extremists are proudly and publicly calling for a violent gender war. Leaders in these movements are coldly weaponizing the trauma of boys and men brutalized by Man

Box culture to drive their ugly political and social agendas. It is an assault on our larger democratic institutions clothed in the rage of sexual frustration and hate. And ultimately, it's nothing new. Women have been the victims of men's sexual frustration and rage throughout the history of the world.

It's well past time for the millions of men to stand up. We must stand and fight for the simple moral imperative that all people are created equal. That all human beings are deserving of autonomy, safety, respect and opportunity, equally. We must break out of Man Box culture and leave our centuries-old domination-based masculinity behind, creating in its place a healthy masculinity of compassion and connection. We must use our power and our privilege to partner with women to heal our world.

And if we continue to fail in this, "Thank you, but no" is all we will ever deserve.

We're All Incels on This Bus

> Because we're raised in Man Box culture, we all
> contain fragments of extremists' world views.
> – February 7, 2020

Lately, I've been writing about incels. Incel stands for involuntary celibate. Incels declare openly that men who don't get selected by women for sex are justified in responding with anger and violence. They wrongly argue that women's choices in sex partners are completely determined by hypergamy – choosing partners based exclusively on bettering their financial or social position, which includes only dating men who are attractive to look at. Incels have committed multiple mass shootings. An incel drove a van onto a busy sidewalk in Toronto, killing ten and injuring sixteen others.

The more I research incels, the more I realize they are not so far removed from the rest of us. The incel worldview arises from the roots of the same tree, our larger culture of masculinity, where all our ideas about how to be a man originate. Incels may exist on that limb "over there" but the idea that the culture of masculinity that created us is also capable of creating them should be deeply troubling to any man reading this.

Incels direct their anger towards Stacys, the idealized and objectified women they can't have because idealized men called Chads get all the best partners for themselves. They see hypergamy as "imprinted on our DNA" and playing out in modern society when women pass them over for men of "higher value." In order to validate their world view, incels must steadfastly refuse to acknowledge men's capacities for healing, connection, growth, empathy, rich emotional expression and, yes, romantic love. They must also view "higher value men" from the narrow and restrictive frame of dominance-based Man Box culture.

How incels and other masculinity extremists construct language is quite telling. Incels talk about higher value men and women controlling the sexual marketplace, language choices that place the miraculous diversity of sexual intimacy firmly in the realm of the transactional. This should come as no surprise, given that our dominance-based culture of masculinity prioritizes roles and status over relationships and values power created over others versus power created with others. The cold mechanics of transactions are the Man Box model for relating to women. "I'll give you what you want if you'll give me sex."

Man Box love, y'all.

Man Box Culture Spawns Masculinity Extremists

So-called Men's Rights Activists (MRAs), Men Going Their Own Way (MGTOWs), and incels represent the best-known incarnations of masculinity extremists. I have coined this term in order to mark their positionality on the outer edges of our larger continuum of masculinity. They, like the rest of us, grew up in our bullying Man Box culture, taught that being a man means never showing emotions (unless it's anger), and means always being dominant, making lots of money, asserting control over women, having lots of sex, never being gay, and so on.

The rules of Man Box culture may vary across different regions and populations, but the exact rules themselves are secondary to Man Box culture's primary purpose. Its purpose is to instill in boys and men the dominance-based model of masculinity, which is authoritarian, moving power and control ever upward on the pyramid of control it maintains. Man Box culture leaves boys and men emotionally traumatized, cut off from connection, vulnerable to being recruited into masculinity extremists' violent views of male victimhood.

There is a direct cause and effect between how Man Box culture polices and bullies boys, and the masculinity extremism, which results. The damage we do to our little sons can be summed up by these two critical factors: 1) We shame and bully boys out of authentic emotional expression and connection. 2) We do this by denigrating the feminine.

We police young boys into hiding their emotions by saying, "What are you, a girl?" or "What are you, a sissy?" In this way, we wrongly gender universal human relational capacities for emotional expression as feminine, and then hammer away at boys with the message that female is less. By the time they reach adolescence, boys have heard messages denigrating their supposedly feminine need for expression and connection dozens of times every day.

Eventually, they give up their close friendships in order not to be seen by other boys as "a little kid, girly or gay." This leads to a lifetime of isolation. And because the denigration of the feminine is central to how we police boys into isolation, many of us look right past decades of brutal bullying at the hands of other boys and men and instead blame women, especially feminist women, for our challenges.

It's a blind spot of startling proportions, wherein men avoid unpacking a lifetime of brutality and bullying by other men, but become enraged when women refuse to accept this bullying as well.

There is a massive cognitive dissonance in this moment. Women's rejection of dominance-based masculinity highlights men's refusal to challenge it. We see our own histories of victimhood as perpetrated by other boys and men laid out before us, and unable to face that trauma and shame, we instead attack the messenger, feminism.

As long as our default culture of masculinity is dominance-based, every generation of boys will continue to struggle, expressing their manhood in dangerous and unhealthy ways. Our little sons and grandsons are at risk for disaffected, lonely lives, resulting in the kind of anger and rage that makes them susceptible to extremism of all kinds.

Incels, MRAs and MGTOWs are the canaries in the coalmine of our larger dominance-based culture of masculinity. The distorted rationalizations of incel victimhood are darkly familiar to many of us. Masculinity extremists' rage towards women is a by-product of our larger collective unwillingness to unpack the isolating trauma inflicted on us by Man Box culture. Too easily, scapegoating voices whisper in the back of all our minds, "Women have all the advantages now. The world isn't fair to men," and so on.

To be an incel, you must declare over and over how ugly a person you are. By sucking up all of the oxygen in the room, the incessant "me, me, me" of incels' self-loathing narrative seeks to obscure a single moral absolute, one that is central to our most basic notions of human autonomy and individual freedom.

No one owes anyone sex.

In a sane society, the right to say "no" to any request for physical or emotional intimacy is paramount. Men's collective failure to respect this moral absolute in every single interpersonal

118

exchange we initiate is what is fueling the white-hot core of the #MeToo movement. Meanwhile, women are becoming more powerful. They and the men who are their allies are creating a world where abusive men are being challenged. This is leading to a crisis in dominance masculinity. Angry, retrogressive voices are calling for open war against women, LGBTQ people, people of color, immigrants, religious minorities and others, and the outcome of this battle is by no means guaranteed to go well. It is an assault on our larger democratic institutions clothed in the rage of sexual frustration and hate. And ultimately, it's nothing new. Girls and women have been survivors of men's sexual frustration and violence throughout the history of the world.

Masculinity extremists are the result of Man Box culture. Our Man Box culture. A culture that will not go away until hundreds of millions of men make the conscious choice to replace our Man Box culture with a healthy masculine culture of connection and compassion.

Not only is this one on us, gentlemen. This one is us.

Domination Culture is What the Republican Party is Selling

> We're up against a deadly dangerous enemy, and
> we're still asking the wrong questions.
> – August 26, 2020

As the Republican Party leans more and more into what seem to be impossibly contradictory positions, we need to understand that Trump's base isn't about what's rational. It's about the visceral pleasure of domination.

It was repellent to me when, during the 2016 primary, Trump created nasty little nicknames for every other GOP candidate. Back then, the first time I heard him call Marco Rubio "Little Marco" I was disgusted. This was straight up playground bully talk. One simple act would have changed everything in the 2016 primary: If Marco Rubio or Ted Cruz, whose wife Trump openly insulted, had walked over and punched Trump in the face on national television. But they did not. They took the bullying, were cowed, and Trump became president.

What we saw was how bullying in domination-based masculinity determines status in that hierarchy. Every existing understanding of political decorum, however frayed it may have already been by decades of Fox News disinformation, went out the window when Trump went full playground bully on national TV.

Trump's domination-based "Make America Great Again" supporters live by a simple set of rules. One punch in the face, and Trump would have been seen as vulnerable and weak, as a clown or a fool who can't back up his words. Instead, something very different happened.

It's time we understood what MAGA authoritarians love about Trump. The national debt is bad? Or is it good? It actually doesn't matter. Which argument gives an authoritarian like Trump the advantage today? That's the argument he'll use. If it changes tomorrow, all the better.

Jerry Falwell, Jr. gets caught in a compromising sexual situation? He will be back. It is hypocritical for evangelicals to have him return? Domination culture thrives on hypocrisy, on chaos, on creating rage in those who oppose it. Its primary goal is to create chaos. As such, hypocrisy is the core expression of domination culture. Domination in all its forms is now the defining Republican Party "value." Seeing this will allow us to understand the threat we face.

A.R. Moxon writes: "So: attacking the very form of voting they themselves enjoy and utilize is indeed hypocrisy, but it's entirely consistent with the only true fascist value, which is domination. Without the hypocrisy, how can you tell you're truly dominating others?"

My work is about our domination-based culture of masculinity. I write about the links between masculinity extremism and white nationalism, racism, sexism, religious intolerance, and more. It all comes down to an appetite for dominance bred into us via trauma inflicted by a culture of disconnection. The path that got us here has been incremental, rooted in the Southern Strategy when Republicans began to build a base among disaffected Southern racists. It was dramatically accelerated when Republican strategist Roger Ailes took over Fox News 1996.

People pose the question, what would make working class Republicans consistently vote against their own interests? That's the wrong question. The question is, how do we fight a culture based entirely on dominating others? Because that's MAGA culture. And this is the end game.

MAGA voters don't care about what's rational. They don't care about what's coming next. They don't care about anything but supporting Trump-style "strong man" authoritarians, creating chaos and brutalizing others. Domination culture has traumatized them and only by traumatizing others can they feel validated. Trump's MAGA is not a political movement. The GOP's authoritarian agenda is to foster a constant cycle of domination-based violence, aligned with white and male supremacist domestic terrorism, compromised Republican politicians, and its vast right wing media networks. The end game is here.

Men and Transactional Intimacy

> Men and women deserve better than a masculine culture of
> dominance that churns out broken men.
> – September 3, 2020

Our generations-old, dominance-based Man Box culture of masculinity shames and bullies young boys out of authentic emotional expression and connection, and then slots them into a hierarchical, pecking order version of masculinity based on a narrow set of rules for being a man.

And what do we call boys who fail to conform to these Man Box culture rules for being a man? We call them sissies, girls, or gay. This drumbeat denigration of the feminine keeps young boys in the Man Box, stripping them of connection even as it teaches them women are less. Because Man Box culture is about what we do, not who we are, men must prove they are living up to these rules every day. Man Box culture doesn't care who we are. It only cares that we can dominate others and rise in status or fail to dominate others and lose status.

This status-driven metric for being a man is deeply transactional. Men's mechanism for self-validation is based on a combination of showing what we have produced and dominating those around us. Whomever scores highest wins. And someone always has to lose. That's how domination-based hierarchies work.

One result is the masculinity extremists' (involuntary celibates and Men's Rights Activists) openly transactional view of human intimacy. They declare human intimacy to be an exchange of goods.

Status for sex, etc. This is a by-product of our domination-based Man Box culture of masculinity. Incels and MRAs talk constantly about the "sexual marketplace" as the mechanism by which women determine who gets to make the transaction for sex and who does not. "Chads, the ideal men, get sex, the rest of us don't."

All of this dysfunction is the result of deep trauma inflicted on young boys, beginning in infancy.

Author and social activist bell hooks writes:

The first act of violence that patriarchy demands of males is not violence toward women. Instead patriarchy demands of all males that they engage in acts of psychic self-mutilation, that they kill off the emotional parts of themselves. If an individual is not successful in emotionally crippling himself, he can count on patriarchal men to enact rituals of power that will assault his self-esteem.

What bell hooks so eloquently describes as "psychic self-mutilation" and "emotional crippling" points to the deeply traumatizing experience boys and men face. What level of ongoing brutality does it take for boys, by late adolescence, to give up the joyful connection of our youth?

All boys and men have left is a culture of masculinity obsessed with transactions. I have no value as an individual, but here is my money, my status, my ability to dominate. What will you trade me for it? Or even worse, what can I take from you?

Men and women deserve better than a masculine culture of bullying and dominance that churns out broken men, angrily spewing their trauma as narratives of bitter transactional disappointment. Human connection is never a transaction. It transcends everything Man Box culture teaches.

My Son, Coronavirus and the Man at the Hot Dog Cart

#FlattenTheCurve and other relevant matters.
– March 13, 2020

My son approaches a hotdog cart in New York City today. He tells the older-aged man operating the cart, "I only have a dollar, can I get a hotdog?" The man says "No, it's not enough." My son starts to walk away. The man says, "Wait, come back."

The man says to my son, "A lot of old people will die soon. Remember me." Then he gives my son a hotdog. My son is 14 years old when he calls me today to tell me this happened.

Sexism is a Gateway Drug to White Supremacy

One predicts the other. Bank on it.
— December 15, 2020

Show me the degree to which a man thinks women are less and you will have shown me the degree to which he is racist. One predicts the other. Bank on it.

In Man Box culture, we teach boys the rules of being a man. The first thing we teach boys is "women are less." We do this by policing boys' and men's masculinity via the denigration of the feminine. This begins shortly after infancy and goes on continually thereafter. (What are you, a girl? What are you, a sissy?)

Eventually, boys under constant bullying and pressure to live up to Man Box culture's expectations engage in public harassment and denigration of women as a shortcut to masculine confirmation.

For boys and men, the dangers of acknowledging, much less advocating for women within our social circles is well known to us. There are terrible and dark sides to the world of men, where alpha males display their strutting locker room dominance, daring any to challenge their open contempt for women, before blithely heading home to their wives and daughters to sit down for Sunday dinner. In this way, generations of men have been bullied into averting our eyes from the ugly and abusive duality of our relationship with women. But it is precisely the dark disdain for women, threaded through our initiation into manhood, that has led us all to #MeToo.

Once we train boys to think their gender makes them better than girls, it's not much of a reach to convince them they're better than others based on race, religion, immigration status, and so on. It's why masculinity extremists and white supremacists are the same population.

Our dominance-based Man Box culture of masculinity teaches boys that girls and women are less, while bullying and shaming boys out of authentic connection and community. Our sons end up emotionally isolated, disaffected, angry, and ripe for recruitment into white nationalism.

All of our society's problems are born out of our generations-old, dominance-based culture of masculinity. Until we replace it with a culture of masculine connection, we will continue to create broken men who do themselves and others harm.

The Conversation, Walking Together, That Didn't Happen

> Acknowledging growth and change in others is
> what unconditional love looks like.
> – September 15, 2019

This article was co-written in conversation with my partner, Dr. Saliha Bava.

Thinking about this today …

Relationships are emergent, co-creative spaces where human beings evolve. If men or women enter into a relationship thinking they already know what an entire relationship needs to be, it's a recipe for atrophy and stasis. Put bluntly, a partner who seeks to define their spouse is a controlling child.

To undo this tendency we all have, to make relationships secure by defining them as consistent and predictable, we should probably just get married again (or not) every year. If we're up for another year, we would state our vows anew, because that's how quickly we are changing and growing. "I'm not who I was." For better or for worse, we co-create in our relationships who each of us is becoming next.

This holds true for children and parents, brothers and sisters, spouses, friends, co-workers and so on. We are becoming who we will become next, in the minute-by-minute back and forth of relating. It's incredibly empowering to think in this way because it allows us to change course and do better in each passing moment.

We grow our relational intelligence when we care for the ways in which we are shaped and changed, ourselves and others, in the powerful process of relating. Acknowledging the power of our moment-by-moment utterances, gestures, words, expression and tone, we define a relationship as a dynamic space instead of a static thing; in which what and who we are is forever emerging.

What is remarkable is that our relationships continue to form who we are, even when some individuals are long gone. A grandparent no longer living can continue to inform who we are becoming, as we change and then reconsider what we experienced with them from a new perspective. Acknowledging and supporting that constant process of growth and change in others, even when it threatens to shift our own constructions of life, is what unconditional love looks like.

Doing otherwise is often at the root of failed relationships. When we, for example, marry and then seek safety and control by trying to keep that person emotionally, professionally, socially forever preserved in that one moment in time, we create ever-increasing tension between our reliance on predictability and the actual truth of their evolving humanity.

The person we profess to love will change, evolve, while we remain fixed on the starting point where they once stood. Whatever the reason for our need for rigid predictability, whether we fear change, or relating, or our own insecurities, the growing distance between our need to keep that person as they were, and our partner's becoming who they are becoming, eventually breaks the lingering connection.

We look up one day from the spot we are fixated on, the spot where our partner or child was ten years ago, and they have walked away over the hill and are gone from sight. What could have been a rich conversation full of new discoveries and change, walking together, didn't happen.

Seeing just how vast the human potential for daily and hourly change is, should never be seen as a threat to us. Change, emergence, growth, is the natural human state of being. We can instead choose to see an endless universe of possibility right there in our partners, our friends, our children. There can be so much excitement, reward and hope. All we need do is walk forward together.

The Pitfalls of Believing Ourselves "Good Men"

A few helpful social media tips for us fellers.
– April 11, 2021

Men who consider themselves "good men" but who instantly default to a defensive posture when challenged by women should self-reflect on why we're so obsessed with being right instead of learning more. We can learn to not do that. I had to. Given my line of work, I had to get used to being wrong. Now, I mess up on Twitter or in an article. I get called out. I own it. Apologize. Learn. Tis human.

The simple fact is, as men, we can never fully comprehend the vast and nuanced ways women get silenced, spoken over, harassed, abused, and assaulted. Too many times I've spoken up in space where women were talking about men without understanding the tone, context, wider implications of the moment. This is where most of my learning takes place. My blind spots also apply to race, sexual identity, gender non-binary folks, immigrants, other religions and so on. If these are not my lived experiences, then I'm never going to completely understand, I can only attempt to.

Yes, it's embarrassing to try and be supportive of a woman's tweet, statement or article, and then find out from women that we've just added to the problem. But too many times I've seen men flip to anger instantly in that moment. Those men have a LOT of personal work to do.

Some of the mistakes I made?

1) Restating the same thing a woman said, in a long-winded

way, thinking I'm expanding on it or being supportive (a version of talking over)

2) Implying I understand something a man can never understand

3) Engaging with a woman who is traumatized and JUST. NEEDS. TO. VENT.

I'm confident women can better list "good man" mistakes. I remain blind to many of them. But I'm learning how to de-center myself and be a witness to what women need to tell us. Translate that to what BIPOC, LGBTQI+ people, even what my own child is trying to tell me. The result? It activates my human compassion and connection. We're never done becoming "good men." There is too much in the world daily dragging us back into a culture of dominance-based masculine behaviors. The best we can do is a daily practice, a mindfulness that centers connection and relationships over roles and status.

Learn to listen first, brothers. Prove we can. Foster trust. Be invited in. When we misstep in those spaces, admit it. Offer an apology. It's not so hard. Exchange humility for our fear of ever being wrong. Take a breath. Grow. It's a beautiful world if we just stop trying to dominate every interaction.

A Simple #MeToo Thought Experiment for Men

Far too many men are choosing to doubt the #MeToo movement.
— June 14, 2020

This thought experiment is for men, especially those of us who have yet to openly and actively take up the work against the sexual abuse and assault of women by speaking out in our personal and professional circles of influence.

This thought experiment is also potentially triggering for rape victims and those sensitive about rape language, so please go forward with care.

But first, this: In the National Intimate Partner and Sexual Violence Survey, the U.S. Centers for Disease Control and Prevention reports that "Approximately 1 in 5 (21. 3% or an estimated 25. 5 million) women in the U.S. reported completed or attempted rape at some point in their lifetime." Sexual assault and harassment are worse for women and gender non-binary people who are Black, Indigenous, and people of color. Given that most sexual assault survivors don't report their attacks, the number is much higher.

That said, I ask men to consider this thought experiment:

Imagine ten women you know personally. Statistically, two of them are likely to be rape survivors. Which two? We don't know, do we? Now, imagine your child's or any child's classroom. Picture any ten of those little girls. Which two of them will be rape survivors? Or perhaps already are? Are we there, yet? Are we feeling a little sick? Because this is the place men need to get to on #MeToo.

Sadly, millions of men accept that denigrating, abusing and attacking women is just part of our culture of masculinity. "It's just the way things are." Some among us are working to create a new culture of masculinity based on the simple moral imperative that all human beings: male, female and non-binary, are deserving of equal rights, protection, opportunity, and dignity; including the simple dignity of being able to walk down our streets without fear.

If you are a man who has not yet taken a clear and public stand against the harassment, abuse, sexual assault and rape of women and non-binary people, ask yourself three questions:

What's your reason for staying silent?

If you remain silent who else will be harmed?

When you remain silent, how do you feel about yourself?

If you don't like your answers then make the choice to end your silence on sexual harassment and assault. Join us. Help us end all forms of sexual assault against women, men, girls and boys.

Be the change you know we all need.

All The Way to Midnight

We were liberated to march with Proud Boys and Oath Keepers, our
creeping panic weaponized into authoritarian rage.
– November 9, 2022

More than half of Boomers fueled the MAGA movement and now the bell curve is descending. The MAGA movement, based on aging white conservative boomer victimhood is now a descending bell curve. Boomers, of which I am one, are dying off. Yet, for the moment, far too many of us are still driving the MAGA movement. How we got here is a combination of our own disconnection, and the vulnerability that disconnection created to decades of carefully crafted political manipulation.

Boomers were wholly unprepared for the manipulations of Fox News in the universal bundled cable of the 90s. White boomers never faced the great depression, or a world war, yet we were particularly susceptible to the idea that we were victims of hardships. In part because of the restless disconnection of our gated community lives we bought fragile white victimhood hook, line and sinker.

After lifetimes of leaning into consumerism and mass consumption we boomers woke up to find ourselves angry and reactive to our own disconnection. Maybe a bigger SUV would help? Maybe a third marriage? That sense of disconnection was a warning, an inflection point. Some of us self reflected. Took stock.

But many more of us doubled down on our nagging sense of victimhood. "Whatever the fuck is wrong here, it must be someone else's fault. Women. Immigrants. Black people." And Fox News was there to lovingly encourage our blind entitlement. To sell us our own failed white fragility.

The MAGA bell curve peaked as we moved into retirement, staring blankly at our own mortality. Because we had bought into the decades long drumbeat of individualism sold to us by a GOP bent on eliminating social safety nets, we sought validation in class and status and so ended up without community.

Retirement is when a strange unnamed panic really set in for boomers. No longer able to rely on the stale connection of surface level workplace relationships, we were left sitting alone in our easy chairs staring at the Tucker Carlsons of the Fox News rabbit hole. Again, it was an inflection point for some of us.

Some boomers said, "Maybe this creeping anxiety is my fault. Maybe this disconnection from my kids, my community, from the world right outside my door is my fault." Some of us went looking for basic human connection. We realized we had been tricked into choosing disconnection. But so many more of us just got angrier.

Trump is the ongoing final act of angry white boomers. No longer did we have to coyly perform the wink wink of coded racist language about welfare queens and urban crime. We were liberated to march with Proud Boys and Oath Keepers, our creeping panic weaponized into authoritarian rage.

There is a fundamental dynamic at play in boomers who are all in on QAnon and MAGA. Each of us saw the off-ramps. We saw the moments in our relatively easy lives when we could've made a different choice, moved toward human connection. What's creeping up on us is now is how late it has become.

For MAGA boomers to admit now, at this terribly late date,

that all the white privilege and rage in the world isn't calming our loneliness or our growing panic, means looking back on 70 years or more and admitting we fell prey to our most selfish, ugly, bullying instincts.

You want to talk terrifying? It is the archetypal Dickens moment. The final inflection point. Scrooge utterly alone staring at everything he values and realizing they are chains. The king MAGA boomer is Donald Trump. Doubling down on rage and dominance all the way to midnight.

To my brothers, sisters and non-binary friends who have already heeded one of the many the inflection points and moved into diverse connection and community, thank you for your courage. To those still flailing amidst the mad contradictions of our fading generation? You can change. You can take the inflection point. It is never too late to do our work and change. But whatever we choose, our days are numbered, and the midterms were proof of it. Our numbers are in decline. We boomers are exiting. Our influence is thankfully, ending. Including my own.

If I have left the impression I'm calling all boomers MAGA, I apologize. I often write about the failings of men only to bring down on myself the "not all men" response when my goal is to address behaviors that trend in populations but don't define all that are in it.

If I have any single goal here, it is to invite self-reflection about the deep social disconnection inherent in our boomer cohort as well as the generations that followed. This disconnection directly contributed to the anxiety and anger of those of us who have fallen prey to the manipulations of the MAGA movement.

Whatever casual dismissals corporate media cares to assign it, the 2022 midterms are an historic inflection point in the pro democracy movement. Young American voters across race and gender have entered the chat. A sitting President and his party held its ground in a midterm for the first time in decades.

An Open Letter to Incels

We've all felt the anger you are feeling.
-January 16, 2020

A self-identified Incel tweeted that not getting sex creates anger, and since women generally control access to sex, it creates general anger toward women. Given the wide proliferation of this challenging narrative, I want to respond. What I want to address is our culture's ongoing validation, if not open encouragement of male anger. Why this validation exists and what it is doing to us.

To the boys and men who identify as incels:

First and foremost, understand you have been raised in man box culture. This dominant culture of masculinity is hierarchical, bullying based, and its number one rule is "don't show your emotions, except for anger." From birth, whenever you showed emotions, you were bullied and shamed for it. Sadness, fear, pain, giddy joy, need for friendship, love, all of this was shamed. And it was shamed via the denigration of the feminine. IE: "What are you, a girl? What are you a sissy?"

The ability to express emotionally in nuanced ways is a key component for connecting in authentic relationships with others, friends, co-workers, romantic partners, everyone. Because of the bullying enforcement of man box culture, you were blocked from growing the capacity for nuanced emotional expression and the authentic connection that creates. We all were.

Instead of having the years of trial-and-error work required to grow our emotional self-regulation/expression, boys in man box culture are blocked from doing this work. Fundamental human capacities for relational connection are wrongly gendered as female, shamed, and blocked. And BECAUSE our bullying man box culture polices boy's emotional expression by denigrating the feminine daily if not hourly, we get bombarded with messages that both strip us of crucial human capacities for connection and condition us to see women and the feminine as less.

The emotional volatility you feel as part of the incel movement is a direct result of being raised in man box culture, which encourages anger as the only acceptable emotional response for men. An emotional response created, not coincidentally, by a lifetime of being bullied and blocked emotionally in man box culture. It's an anger generating closed loop and it is a killer.

Man box culture: "We're going to screw you over emotionally and then we're going aim your resulting isolation, grief and anger at women."

It's all about the anger. Anger when we don't get sex is the same as anger when we don't get anything else we want. As human beings, our job is to manage our baser emotions and grow emotionally to the point where people don't feel they are spending time with someone who is unable to emotionally self-regulate. But because man box culture shames emotional expression, most of us never get the opportunity to do the trial-and-error work over a period of years that we humans need to learn to self-regulate emotionally and to form relationships in nuanced, authentic ways.

144

The relational capacities all humans need to develop are EXACTLY the capacities the man box suppresses in us.

So, if you want to be angry, be angry at every bullying, alpha male jerk that rode you and is still riding you to stay in the man box and hide your authentic self. But understand, the trauma they are dishing out was dished out to them. They're just trying to get far enough up the pecking order to survive. But it's illusory. Because man box culture is domination based, it is inherently isolating, and isolation is what kills us.

And even if you do redirect your anger at the people enforcing man culture that will just be more anger expressed, unless you use that anger to drive self-reflection and change.

Anger resulting from a lack of sex is likely tied to a LOT of other interpersonal emotional trauma rooted in our families of origin and our histories. Trust me, men of my generation have all had to deal with rage and family of origin shit. What we didn't have was an Incel movement telling us "It's right to be angry at women." Feeding on our anger never helps. It won't heal our issues of family of origin nor help us learn to create healthy relationships. We must use our anger to drive our emotional self-work. Otherwise, we're just validating and growing our root emotional trauma.

I have felt what you feel, the same anger and isolation, but I will not let man box culture encourage me to make those ugly emotions the root of my identity. Incel culture is the opposite of the authentic human connection boys and men need. Incel culture is doing to you what has always been done. Blocking you.

And here's a little secret. You're not so different from most the other men walking around today. We're all dealing with trauma and feeling the frustrations you feel. We're all under the thumb of man box culture.

The good news is you can break out of the man box whenever you are finally sick and tired enough of being lonely that you are ready to do the work. Men are waiting to do the work with you. Reach out to The Mankind Project or another men's group. The anger and loneliness we all have felt can end.

And remember this: The next time someone encourages you to hate on any group of people, to feed on and grow your anger, ask yourself what's in it for them. There are many powerful influences in the world that benefit from validating and directing your rage and grief. But they don't give shit about you.

Your brothers at The Mankind Project and other men's groups do care about you. We care about creating a community of brothers, we care about healing our grief and trauma. We care about living rich, connected lives and we can help you do the same. First, see the culture. Then, change the culture.

Understand, Incels are just the tip of the iceberg. The entire population of men have been bombarded with man box bullying and violence. Millions of men, maybe all of us, are stripped of our relational capacities for connection and some of us claw our way back. Be one of those.

I wish you peace, brothers.

Misogyny vs. Misandry: One Has Historically Defined the Structural, One Has Not

> Misandry then, is women's anger against their oppressors.
> Misogyny is men's anger against those they oppress.

– May 23, 2022

Before we begin: Abusive and violent behavior is not limited to men, especially in intimate relationships. The US Centers for Disease Control estimates that about 1 in 4 women and nearly 1 in 10 men have experienced contact sexual violence, physical violence, and/or stalking by an intimate partner during their lifetime and reported some form of IPV-related impact. Over 43 million women and 38 million men have experienced psychological aggression by an intimate partner in their lifetime. You can learn more about the CDC's intimate partner violence data here.

According to the Webster Dictionary, some people hate women and some people hate men. Taken simply in terms of their definitions, misogyny and misandry can appear to be equal and opposite ideas. "Both sides are doing this," and so on. But when we look at these terms through the lens of systems and structures, we see the context and history in which each idea has emerged.

It's an important to understand the power of so called "systems thinking" as there are well-funded, well-organized efforts afoot to restrict us from examining systems and structures across a range of social issues. Refusing to acknowledge or discuss how systems and structures impact our lives is an intentionally political act. This insulates those systems and structures from change. Out of sight is, in fact, very much out of mind.

Discursive processes, that is, the conversations that make up our social relationships, have the power to shift the systemic and structural. Open and robust conversations about systems and structures can shift them in positive ways.

This is why the Republican Party is so focused on silencing the teaching of the racism, or sexism or sexual identity. They are actively demonizing so-called Critical Race Theory because conversations about race are one way to put a spotlight on the long standing systems (the felt but often invisible larger processes) and structures (codified systems which have become sedimented into institutional practices) that are sustaining economic and physical violence against women, BIPOC, LGBTQI+ people, immigrants, people of non-Christian faiths and more.

Acknowledging systems and structures represents a powerful tool for locating where power resides. It can illuminate the where, how and why of confusing or contentious issues. It can help us see who is leveraging conflict and for what purpose. We can apply exactly this systems thinking frame to misogyny and misandry.

Misogyny (hatred of women) is demonstrated in the most explicit ways by male supremacists, members of clearly visible social political movements with leaders, literature, and funding. In an article titled Male Supremacy from the Southern Poverty Law Center, we see that male supremacists and white supremacists have clear overlap in their memberships and share recruitment with each other. Like white supremacy, male supremacy is a product of our dominance-based culture of masculinity, a system which enforces longstanding structural advantages embedded in legal, religious and institutional advantages to keep white men at the top of its strict hierarchy. Another term for this system of power and advantages for men is patriarchy.

Women and non-binary people are fighting back against men's systemic advantages, demanding equity in the workplace, seeking legal redress in the courts, and calling for physical safety and autonomy. While this is increasing power for women, there is no historic female equivalent of patriarchy, which created generations of systemic and structural legal oppression against men by women. That never happened and isn't happening now.

(White) men have always had the right to own property, vote, and engage in financial transactions. Women have not. For example: Until the Equal Credit Opportunity Act in 1974, women needed their husband's signature to get a credit card. It wasn't until the signing of the Women's Business Ownership Act of 1988, that federal law put an end to state laws that required women to have male relatives sign business loans.

To this day, fundamentalist Christian churches as well as other faiths define women as subservient to men. There has never been a major world religion that defines men as subservient to women.

In the US, long standing systemic, coordinated subjugation of women by fundamentalist Christian extremists is playing out right now with the overturn of Roe v. Wade. Laws have already been passed in Texas and other states, forcing underage girls and women to take pregnancies to term, even in the case of rape, incest or medically dangerous pregnancies. Collectively, men's failure to stop this systemic attack on women's rights and autonomy speaks volumes to our collective indifference to the impact we have on women's lives. It's happening because collectively men are passively letting it happen or actively encouraging it to happen.

Men's Rights Activists and other male extremists point to our family courts as equivalent levels of systemic or structural disadvantages for men. Such supposed disadvantages are born out generations of neglect and abuse by fathers. Prior to our current family court system, men walked away from their families at a time when women were also kept out of the workplace, leaving mothers to fend for themselves and their children with no resources.

My own grandfather, walked out on my father's family in 1930's depression era Richmond, Virginia. There was no family court to require he pay child support, and so, my grandfather went his own way, starting another family a few counties away. The resulting impact on the life of my three-year-old father, his mother and his younger sister was catastrophic. What takes place in the family courts is legal redress for long histories of wrongdoing by men against mothers and children. I have been through that system myself, having been divorced from the mother of my then four year old child.

It was not fun, but what it required of me on behalf of my son was easy enough to understand.

From child marriage across the US, to acid attacks in India, to epidemic levels of domestic violence, rape and femicide against women globally, to ongoing efforts to block women from leadership roles in business and politics, to the war against abortion, the list of inequities against women is global, generational and ongoing. If there is widespread anger and resentment against men by women and non-binary people, it is born out of generations of ongoing systemic violence and oppression directed by men against those populations. Put simply, no one likes their abuser.

150

Which begs the question, what then is misogyny, the hatred of women, born out of? In the absence of an equal and opposite history of systemic and structural inequities leveraged by women against men, what is the source of men's anger toward women? Using a systemic/structural lens, which can be applied to track power in hierarchies, misandry and misogyny are both seen to be rooted in a single source: in how we train boys into our dominance-based culture of masculinity.

In dominance-based masculinity, otherwise known as Man Box culture, we bully boys beginning in infancy out of emotional expression and connection. When a boy shows emotion or too much need for connection, he is bullied back into the Man Box by questioning his masculinity. (What are you a sissy? What are you a girl?) In this way, we train our young sons out of universal human relational capacities such as empathy, care-giving, compassion, and connection across difference, slotting them instead into our dominance-based hierarchical culture of masculinity in which we must dominate those around us in order to maintain our status and validate our masculinity. If we fail to do so, we lose status. The result is a culture of ongoing policing, bullying and violence. Those boys and men who stray too far from the strict rules of Man Box culture are murdered.

Boys are systemically bullied into lifetimes of loneliness and disconnection via the ongoing denigration of the feminine. In this way, we are also taught daily, even hourly, that girls and women are less. Most of this anti-female conditioning is cemented in place before we are even old enough to know what is happening.

For boys and men, misogyny isn't a reaction to systemic oppression by women, it is the result of Man Box culture, which requires we denigrate girls and women daily in order to validate our masculinity. In Man Box culture we are expected to display power over women and girls.

The ongoing oppression of women is enshrined in religious, legal, political, educational, and employment systems and structures. An equivalent level of systemic and structural oppression has not been experienced by the current generation of white men in America. Meanwhile, women's healthcare and bodily autonomy are under renewed attack with the reversal of Roe v. Wade. In this we can see the ongoing systemic and structural assault against women's rights playing out in real time. There is no equivalent loss of rights for men.

Misandry then, is women's anger against their oppressors. Misogyny is men's anger against those they oppress.

MRAs, Incels and other male supremacists seek to give the word misandry parity with misogyny, declaring their own victimhood as part of a fundamental strategy common to extremists of all stripes. It can be defined in its most brutal terms as "the act of stabbing someone while loudly declaring they are stabbing you." When white and male supremacists amplify victimhood frames, IE: "we are being erased," they grant themselves permission to do violence. "Look what you made me do."

Violence up to and including genocide against underrepresented groups becomes widespread and normalized in cultures and societies where the critical examination of the systems and structures, which control our lives, has been silenced. In the US, look for the Republican Party to continue to shut down all teaching and discussion of race, gender, sexual identity, and religious bigotry.

False equivalencies and weaponized victimhood are effectively countered by discussions of systems and structures. The discursive, the process of discussing the systems and structures that impact our lives, gives us the power to shift those structures to make a better world.

Too Many Women Are Going to College!

This is how male victimhood works.
September 14, 2021

There's a male supremacist narrative out there that increasingly more women are going to college than men because of educational bias, unfair advantages, and so on. Just like every other male supremacy talking point, it's based on a male victimhood narrative, cuz that's how male supremacy works.

These narratives always have a grain of truth. Yes, boys are struggling in many educational contexts. Yes, a lot of programs have been implemented to encourage women in STEM and other areas. Fine. We get that. We need to address what's going on for boys. Thanks for that grain.

But why do women gravitate towards education? First and foremost, women and non-gender binary people pursue education because there is great joy for all humans in exploring the issues and ideas we're interested in.

But there's another reason why girls and women pursue education.

Globally, girls and women pursue education at whatever level is available to them to gain financial and personal independence from controlling men. Education is freedom for women. *Full stop.*

Patriarchal power over women is counteracted by higher levels of education in every possible way. From freeing women from the need to be married, to allowing women's ability to choose work that is meaningful and validating for them, to their increased ability to demand fair and equal pay.

And yet, when I say this some man drops in to say… "This is total crap. Every woman in college didn't go there to get away from the controlling men in their families." Some men say things like this because millions of us are oblivious to the larger systems and structures which advantage us. Patriarchal power and control systems that have been in place for generations? That detail goes right over our heads.

So, to be clear: A global context of systemic sexism across every aspect of women's personal and professional lives is driving girls' and women's focus on education. They pursue education to whatever degree is allowed them by systems that still seek to control them.

For example: Women being introduced for the first time in business meetings will often add their level of education to their job title as part of how they introduce themselves. This is something men don't need to do. Women do so to get men to respect them when they speak during the meeting. Additionally, women pursue education as leverage to negotiate equal pay for equal work. "You aren't hiring a woman, you're hiring a PhD."

MRA's and other masculinity extremists are pointing to the 57% higher college enrollment for women as proof the education system is increasingly biased against men. The implication is higher enrollment for women is something new. It is not.

From the New York Times:

> "Women have outnumbered men on campus since the late 1970s. The ratio of female to male undergraduates increased much more from 1970 to 1980 than from 1980 to the present. And the numbers haven't changed much in recent decades. In 1992, 55 percent of college students were women. By 2019, the number had nudged up to 57.4 percent.

156

While the shift in the college gender ratio is often characterized as men 'falling behind,' men are actually more likely to go to college today than they were when they were the majority, many decades ago. In 1970, 32 percent of men 18 to 24 were enrolled in college, a level that was most likely inflated by the opportunity to avoid being drafted into the Vietnam War. That percentage dropped to 24 percent in 1978 and then steadily grew to a stable 37 percent to 39 percent over the last decade."

And finally, men have always been able to make a decent living in trades like plumbing and construction. Careers that women have traditionally been kept out of. Which goes a long way to explain the college disparity. Men choose to not go to college. Women have few alternative options.

Male supremacist falsehoods designed to drive men's victimhood narratives cherry pick data and then invite boys and men to set aside self-reflection, accountability for their own choices, critical thinking and cultural awareness and collapse into white and male supremacy.

My suggestion that women chose to pursue education to gain independence from controlling men simply acknowledges women's willingness to work for their own betterment instead of blaming others for their failing to do so.

Would that MRA's had the ability to do the same.

I absolutely agree that we need to support boys' emotional and educational development in ways we are failing to do now. But to get there, we first must stop spinning our wheels on false narratives about unfair educational advantages for girls and women. This is about the harm done to young men by our Man Box culture of masculinity. Until we go hard at what hierarchical, dominance-based masculinity creates in boys' development, the rest is only working the edges of the problem.

For This Generation of Men There Will Be No Resolution

It will likely take a generation or more for us to collectively free ourselves. And that's if we're lucky enough to do it quickly.
– March 15, 2019

I understand why men might feel frustrated. It's a hard piece of news to find out we can't simply shift our personal behavior and call white and male supremacy fixed. It's a dark realization to find out that, despite all our efforts, we have still only scratched the surface of truly understanding the trauma daily being inflicted across the globe on women, on people of color, immigrants and children. It's a shock to get woken up, to understand that humankind's generations of trauma cannot be healed in our lifetimes or even the lifetimes of our children.

We are a generation of men tasked with addressing ongoing, systemic trauma, both others' and ours. We are tasked with taking some personal responsibility for the brutal realizations of #MeToo, #BlackLivesMatter and the ugly outbreak of white supremacy across Europe and America.

Waves of catastrophic trauma are the result of generations of violent, abusive Man Box culture, and because of how Man Box culture has bullied and conditioned men, we have been stripped of the very capacities we need to repair the damage done.

Our culture, the culture we maintain, has suppressed in boys and men our deeply human capacities for empathy, emotional expression, collaboration, and connection.

We have been cheated out of human connection by a culture of manhood that tells us independence is the most vaunted of masculine traits, that hiding our emotions makes us strong, and that dominating those around us is the only course of action that will keep us safe. In the beautiful human experience we have been bullied and brutalized into disconnection and isolation. All in the pursuit of proving we are "real men."

Man Box culture teaches us to never show self-doubt, to never admit we are wrong, to always have the last word. It teaches us to align ourselves with bullying hierarchical power structures as a way to construct our social institutions. It teaches us to rely on power created over others instead of power created with others. But it's a model for human society that is not working. The human experiment is faltering. And so, men's anger surges up in the disconnect between the privileges that we continue to exercise every day, and the calamity that is modern life. Surely this is someone else's fault. Immigrants. Socialists. Feminists.

No. It is not. Our dominance-based culture of masculinity, formed and framed by the Man Box, is entirely responsible for where we are in this moment in history. Which means this is on us, and as hard as it may be to own that, we must own it if we are to save future generations from yet more despair and destruction.

To do this work, we must face basic facts. We have to admit the truth of how desperately disconnected we have become. Even as men rage on in defense of individualism and traditional masculinity, we are experiencing epidemic levels of violence, drug abuse, alcoholism, suicide, and divorce.

We are falling prey to an epidemic of loneliness, and Man Box culture is at the root of our loneliness because it polices and punishes authentic connection.

We must stop denying basic truths. Regardless of how we intersect with others in terms of our individual power, wealth, opportunity and resources, collectively men have always held the levers of power in the world. A cursory glance at the makeup of the U.S. Congress and corporate America will verify this is still absolutely the case.

This makes men responsible for what has happened to women, children, our nation, the economy, our global environment and to all of the diverse communities that make up the human family.

The message we are hearing from men like Tony Porter of A CALL TO MEN couldn't be simpler. We are responsible for our own actions and the actions of other men. No one gets to stay on the sidelines and call himself a good man. If you are not actively opposing the ongoing trauma created by sexist, racist behaviors, you are enabling them.

And the news gets worse. If responsibility for all men isn't enough to take on, we are also responsible for the actions of our fathers, our grandfathers and our great grandfathers, back across generations. Not in terms of deserving punishment for what they did, but in terms of healing the generational trauma generated by their choices. This includes reparations for BIPOC communities. This includes creating organizational cultures of diversity, equity and inclusion, across healthcare, education, governments, religion, corporations and so on, intentionally undoing our cruel and counterproductive systemic advantages. When we fail to do this work, when we do nothing, we remain haunted.

Which is why even as we mow our suburban lawns and drink

our artisanal cocktails, we are shaken by a dark, unnamable anxiety. It's a rolling wave of generational trauma, once hidden from us by our own comfortable privilege. It is a wave that took hundreds of years to form and will take hundreds of years more to spend itself. The current generation of men is at the apex of this wave. Every action we take either adds momentum to this wave of trauma or reduces its impact on the generation that follows us. And because other voices besides ours are growing louder and more insistent, we are all being forced to face this painful realization.

We can no longer play by the old rules, whereby our 1950s-era cultural container made our isolated Man Box lives livable because women, LGBTQ people, and BIPOC had no choice but to play along. As others fight for equity, the cultural container that made possible a society designed to empower only men is fragmenting.

A new culture is emerging. We don't get to know what that one looks like, yet. And we don't get to sidestep. We are the liminal generation. We are the middlemen. We are never going to see the end of the war between the sexes even as we might work to end it. We will not know what peace looks like. The generations of men who came before us have seen to that.

If this feels unfair, it should. But know the world men created is far more unfair to others. No matter how hard we try to be better human beings, we still get to own that towering wave of trauma, because we continue to benefit from the systems that create it. If women are paid less, it's because we are paid more. While people of color are shot dead by police for no other reason than the color of their skin, we are allowed to rage in the street while police quietly talk us down.

My desk, my keyboard, the length of my fingers, the health of my body, the absurd possibility that I can write this article while children are slaughtered in Yemen or Syria, all these things are a direct result of my white male privilege. If we can't acknowledge that fact, then we're adding momentum to the wave; a wave that will crash down on our own grandchildren, be they sons or daughters, white, brown or Black.

There is no one strong leader who will save us. No smart bomb. No tough love. No John Wayne showdown. There is no neutral fix. Simply not adding to the damage won't be enough. None of what our Man Box culture of manhood has taught us will fix a world informed by trauma. We must instead do something new and entirely different. We must witness and help heal the pain of others.

Generations of cultural messages have wrongly gendered connection and empathy as feminine.

Man Box culture has bullied and shamed us into stripping ourselves of the full range of human capacities for compassion and connection. Along with leadership and toughness, we must also embrace community and caregiving. To open ourselves up, to care for the suffering of others, is a step toward the divine.

And so, we must learn the art of being in relationship.

Men must stop making communication about what we want, need or require, and instead make it about holding space for uncertainty, not knowing and what is emerging. The trauma we, and those around us carry, is not something to be quickly resolved. In a world where men have been trained to fix instead of host, repair instead of engage, we must learn to hold space for the full range of human emotions in the back and forth of relating.

We must learn to acknowledge others, ourselves, and a third entity, the shared relationship; an entity that, no matter how hard we try, we can never fully dominate, control or determine. We must accept that others will be out of our control, will hold us accountable, will ask of us patience, compassion and empathy. We have to learn to acknowledge our place in the greater network of our relationships. Only then will what we want in our own lives perhaps be available to us, not by virtue of our privilege, but by virtue of our humanity.

Men are insightful and intuitive creatures. Beneath our stoic Man Box exteriors we are deeply human. We have the capacity to live rich, abundant, connected lives. We can seek and give shelter, form community, express our truths and act with the moral clarity that is always born out of giving care.

Yes, of course, be tough, be strong. These are natural human capacities to be encouraged in our sons and our daughters equally. But reach further. It is in the back and forth of connecting and relating with others that we find our purpose and our meaning. It's well past time for us to bring into play the full range of human capacities that we are all born with. The work of generations is waiting to be done. And the salvation of our species hangs in the balance.

All we have to do is begin.

On Predictive Grief

"Let me try and carry you the way I used to, one more time."
– July 3, 2020

I have a 15-year-old son. He's beautiful and I love him dearly. He will leave our house someday and not live here anymore. The thought of him going is something I grieve years before it's happening. It runs deeper than him going. His childhood is going away. I'm watching him daily begin to shoulder adulthood, like shrugging on a coat to go out in winter, one sleeve at a time. Pulling it on. We owe our children this. To help them do this.

My predictive grief is born in part out of my sense memory of still carrying him in the crook of my arm. His hand resting on the back of my neck as we went about our most important daily business. The past is still right here with me, in the crook of my arm.

I remember a day many years ago, when he was getting taller and I said to him, "Let me try and carry you the way I used to one more time." I lifted him and his chin was eye level to me. We laughed and I put him down after a moment. I recall the weight of him that day.

Predictive grief is the past and the future folding neatly across each other, accordion-like; the past and the future, simultaneously seen from each vantage point.

Did I see myself here writing these words on that day? Some days it feels like decades are one thin fold apart. He is growing and changing. I would never seek to inhibit that. His rising power and his increasing separation from me are things I am encouraging.

This makes me proud, both of my work as a parent and his work as a young person. but also of the love that seeks to remain in place. The love that continues to form itself out of all the confusion that leaving childhood creates. How to hold him now? How do we mend the rifts that time seeks to foster? "I don't know the answers anymore ... Maybe if we talk they will emerge?"

I remember my son sitting in the crook of my arm looking away towards something out beyond me. I take a deep breath and calm the predictive fears that are (possibly) unfounded. His childhood is moving beyond my conscious self into memory, into dreams. That is enough.

Now let us consider what is not predictive grief. Let us consider the moments when his child self appears, giggling. Let us consider the gentle letting go, alongside the eternal invitation of the child in all of us. "Visit any time child." Predictive grief is a poetic lovely pain, yes. Predictive grief reminds us to be mindful of the moment before us. Not to dwell on future losses; to appreciate what we have before us today. What do I have? I have a magical mixture of child and adult right here in my life.

I am blessed to be with him. To remind him in his sometimes uncertainty of how proud I am of him. That when I make a mistake, I can seek his forgiveness. That I am here for him. That he is of me and I of him. Who gets to do this magical thing? Such a gift. Such a gift.

Thank you, predictive grief. You reminded me not to be sitting somewhere twenty years from now wondering why I missed my chance to be here for him today. You remind me of who I want to be someday. The person who loved my boy now.

Men's True Power

> Men's power lies in the deeply human gifts
> we all are born with.

There is a fundamental lesson for men. For those who choose to hear it, to see it, it's always been with us. It's scrawled in the crumbling pages of thousand-year-old spiritual texts, carried aloft on the prayers of countless AA meetings by broken men holding cups of black coffee and their own fear in check. We see it in our children's eyes as they look up at us. It's always been right there. As men, we can come to understand this lesson, but often at great cost, after a crisis of our own making, the loss of our careers or the collapse of a marriage.

Here is that lesson. Our power as men does not lie in how well we can dominate and control those around us. Our culture seeks to convince us otherwise, but our Man Box culture is a formula for never-ending stress to keep proving our manhood coupled with the growing panic of eventual failure. Moreover, it is deeply and fundamentally isolating. And isolation is death. Men's power lies in our natural human capacity to form and care for relationships, to collaborate, share, empathize, and connect, creating meaning and purpose for ourselves, alongside our friends, partners, children and communities. We can create lives in which we feel deeply human and fully alive. We can make the world a safer and more joyful place.

We can leave the anxiety behind. We can be free. A true and lasting sense of security is created not via wealth taken from or power created over others, but in a network of healthy authentic relationships. It is in robust and reliable communities that we resource ourselves during times of personal and professional crisis. This has always been the central purpose of human relationships, to form more stable, secure and rewarding lives in community.

The first step to create this more joyful life is a simple one. We need only admit that we want and need authentic, meaningful connection in our lives. What follows this simple admission is the miracle of being human.

Even if we have been bullied or bullied others, been trained out of forming relationships over the course of a lifetime, the capacity to fully connect remains, just beyond the door, waiting for us to let it back in. And there are men who have done this work, who are waiting to help others among us to open the door.

Good men are working to end Man Box culture, based on the following simple truths. Men do not want to be angry. Men do not want to be alone. Men are not naturally inclined toward the toxic confines of the Man Box. If we were, it wouldn't be killing us. If you have had enough of the Man Box, join us. Groups like The Mankind Project and Humen are tearing down the walls of isolation that trap men in cycles of anger and reactivity. If you are a man who is struggling, who is tired of being alone, reach out to these men, or to other men's groups. Contact a therapist. Get some self-help books.

I will tell you this, when you enter a room full of men who are not judging you, not skeptical of you, not looking to undercut, silence, or reject you, the difference is palpable. It's like breathing free for the very first time. All you have to do is open the door to connection and step through.

168

"When we seek for connection, we restore the world to wholeness."

-Margaret J. Wheatley

MARK GREENE

Consultant, Coach, Author, Speaker

Mark writes, speaks, and consults, on Man Box culture, and relational practices for organizations worldwide. Mark works with organizations and individuals to help them overcome the challenges created by retrogressive, dominance-based business cultures.

Mark is the author of *The Little #MeToo Book for Men*, *Remaking Manhood*, Stories from the Front Lines of Change, and co-author, along with Dr. Saliha Bava, of the *Relational Book for Parenting and The Relational Workplace*. Mark is co-host of Remaking Manhood, the Healthy Masculinity Podcast. You can reach Mark at RemakingMahood.com.

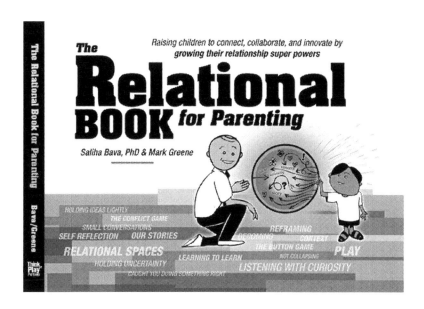

From Mark Greene and Dr. Saliha Bava:

The Relational Book for Parenting - The ability to create healthy, authentic relationships will be the key to our children's personal and professional success over the course of their lifetimes. Co-authors Saliha Bava, PhD and Mark Greene's book is a playful mix of comics, fables, games and powerful hands-on relational ideas. It's a playful path to insure our children's ability to connect, collaborate, and innovate by growing their relationship super powers.

More at ThinkPlayPartners.com

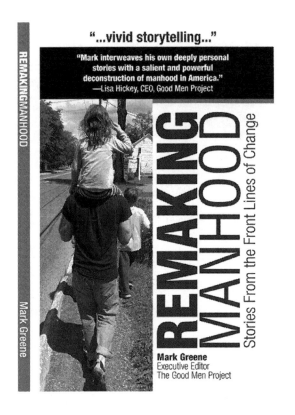

Remaking Manhood is a collection of Good Men Project Senior Editor Mark Greene's most popular articles on parenting, fatherhood and manhood. *Available at* **Amazon**.

"This is writing that unites men rather than dividing or exploiting them. It speaks to the very best part of men and asks them to bring that part to the fore—as fathers, as sons, as brothers, as husbands, as friends, as lovers, and as citizens of life."

—**Michael Rowe, author of Other Men's Sons**

The Little #MeToo Book for Men

In just seventy-five brief pages, Good Men Project Senior Editor Mark Greene exposes the brutal price that man box culture extracts from men and women worldwide. **The Little #MeToo Book for Men** is a concise, no holds barred call to action, inviting men to step out of silence and isolation and into the battle for a better future.

"The Little MeToo Book for Men is a profoundly empathetic guide for men who are navigating a culture that pressures them to give up their humanity. The book is nothing short of a blueprint for men's liberation."

– Caroline Heldman, Ph.D., Executive Director, The Representation Project.

From Mark Greene and Dr. Saliha Bava:

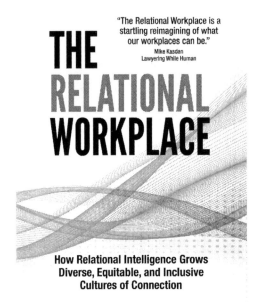

"The Relational Workplace is a startling reimagining of what our workplaces can be."
Mike Kasdan
Lawyering While Human

THE RELATIONAL WORKPLACE

How Relational Intelligence Grows Diverse, Equitable, and Inclusive Cultures of Connection

Saliha Bava, PhD and Mark Greene

In The Relational Workplace, authors Dr. Saliha Bava and Mark Greene draw on decades of organizational, systems, and communication theory, research, and philosophy, to help us create more fully connected working lives. Bava and Greene have written a playful, accessible, and deeply impactful resource for co-creating human connection, especially across the vast range of intersectional differences that define our global human family.

Learn how to **Listen with Curiosity • Consider Context • Stay Playful • Hold Uncertainty • Ask Questions • Reframe Our Stories** and more. Explore **The Relational Discursive Loop, Man Box Culture Choice Point,** and **Culture of Curiosity as Shared Inquiry,** powerful systemic frames for positive organizational ADEI transformation.

More at RelationalWorkplace.com

REMAKING
MANHOOD
The **HEALTHY MASCULINITY** PODCAST
with Mark Greene and Charles Matheus

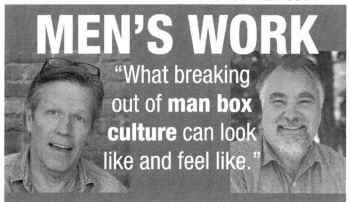

MEN'S WORK
"What breaking out of **man box culture** can look like and feel like."

Remaking Manhood, The Healthy Masculinity Podcast - For generations, our culture has taught us a narrow limiting set of rules for how to be a man. The end result? Epidemic levels of isolation and violence for boys and men and for the multitude of others who's lives we impact.

But we can instead choose a masculinity of connection

and in return have healthier relationships and more meaningful, lasting lives. Every episode you'll hear honest conversations designed to show you what breaking out of the man box can look like and feel like.

Available on your favorite streaming service.

Printed in Great Britain
by Amazon

37871050R00097